Quillir

Flowers

Quilling
Flowers

Sena Runa

THE GUILD OF MASTER CRAFTSMAN
PUBLICATIONS

Contents

Introduction

Paper quilling has a long history that dates back several hundred years. During the Renaissance, nuns and monks would apply gilded paper coils to religious icons instead of gold and silver in an effort to save money. When the paper quilling was gilded, it was hard to distinguish from costly metals. The style of quilled designs has changed significantly over the past few decades and paper quilling has become very popular in recent years.

It has been more than ten years since I first discovered paper quilling. My intention had been to enjoy it as a hobby alongside my career, but I gained so much satisfaction from it that I soon decided I wanted to focus on it full time.

I love trying out new quilling shapes and techniques, and I find the results are always satisfying because I'm making something unique. An infinite number of designs can be created by adding different shapes alongside the ones used in traditional quilling; you'll find this out for yourself as you work your way through the projects.

In the following pages there's advice on the tools and materials needed, plus all the technical know-how required to create 20 fabulous flower projects. I used all kinds of techniques and shapes to make the quilled flowers look more realistic. For example, by colouring paper strips with a marker, you can replicate the exact shade of a flower's petals.

Flower artworks can make great gifts for friends and family as cards or framed pictures. Some of the projects are also birth flowers so, for example, you could give a water lily artwork to someone who was born in July.

These projects may also inspire to create your own flowers, experimenting with different colours and shapes. There are endless possibilities to enjoy, and I'm sure you'll find it quite addictive.

I am sharing my experience and knowledge here in the hope that I will encourage new and existing quilling devotees, and in so doing, help to continue this wonderful art form. So let's get started!

Sena Runa

Tools & materials

SCISSORS Ⓐ

For quilling, choose a medium-sized pair of scissors with fine pointed ends. You will use them to cut the paper as well as bend it. If you prefer, you can use bigger scissors for cutting the larger pieces of the cardstock, but you will need a smaller pair for detailed cutting.

TWEEZERS Ⓑ

A fine-tipped pair of tweezers are necessary for holding and placing the paper strips and coils, especially for placing the smaller elements. Choose one that feels comfortable while holding in your hand.

CRAFT KNIFE Ⓒ

For cutting paper strips and cardboard, the ideal tool is a craft knife. The blade is replaceable – always make sure you use a sharp blade for the best results.

QUILLING TOOL Ⓓ

You can use a special quilling tool to make coils but it is not essential if you prefer to use your fingers. A quilling tool has a slotted end for holding the end of a paper strip while you turn it to make a coil.

QUILLING NEEDLE Ⓔ

To trace a template outline and lines onto the base, you will need a quilling needle or a similar tool, such as a compass. It is best to use one with a fine-tipped needle, but avoid one that is very sharp, because it may damage the paper when you are tracing. The needle should be hard enough that it doesn't bend under pressure when you press it on the paper.

COPIC MARKER PENS Ⓕ

These pens have a translucent ink, making them perfect for blending colours. They can be used to change the paper's colour to create a desired shade. You will also need one of these, or any other pen, to help make wave shapes in the paper strips.

RULER Ⓖ

A ruler is necessary for checking the size of a strip of paper and to measure the correct length. It's also helpful to check the size of the other shapes that you prepare. For some of the projects in this book, you will need to cut your own strips, and for these it is best to use a metal ruler, as it will provide a firmer edge to cut against with a craft knife.

WHITE GLUE Ⓗ

To stick the shapes onto the base paper, white craft paper glue is recommended as it dries clear and is therefore invisible. Liquid glues are easier to apply and do not dry out in the bottles as quickly. It's also a good idea to choose an easy-to-remove version, as this will enable you to clean your tools and hands more easily.

CRIMPER TOOL Ⓘ

This quilling tool is designed to help you crimp the quilling paper more easily and quickly.

CUTTING MAT Ⓙ

Any cutting mat will be suitable for the projects in this book. A self-healing mat is ideal if you are going to use it for a long period of time or if you are making straight cuts with quite a lot of pressure applied.

PAPER Ⓚ

All the projects in this book are made with ⅜in (1cm) wide quilling paper strips and cardstock strips. For the quilling paper strips, the best weight is 60–90lb (90–135gsm) for coloured acid-free paper; for the cardstock strips, choose 110lb (300gsm) weight. Acid-free paper keeps its colour much longer than other types.

You can either use ready-made quilling sets that include colourful strips, or you can cut your own paper strips at home using a craft knife. The cardstock strips will need to be cut at home using a craft knife. You can use any colours you like for the projects - the ones in this book are just suggestions. For the base that supports the strips, using a heavier paper (150lb/220gsm) or a cardstock (90lb/250gsm) is recommended to prevent it buckling or wrinkling when the glue is applied.

(A)   (B)   (C)   (D)   (E)   (F)   (G)   (H)   (I)   (J)   (K)

Techniques

COIL – USING A QUILLING TOOL

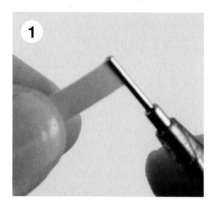
1

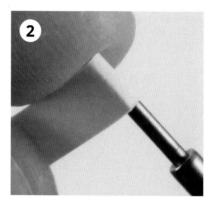
2

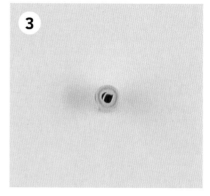
3

Place the edge of a strip of paper into the slot at the end of the quilling tool.

Twirl the quilling tool while you hold the end of the paper strip tightly with your other hand. To keep the coil straight, push the side of it gently as you twirl.

When you finish twirling the paper, you should have a coil that looks like the one shown here. Hold it with one hand tightly and pull the tool out.

COIL – USING YOUR FINGERS

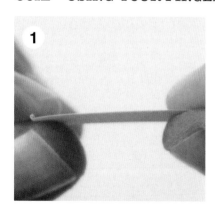
1

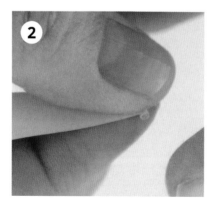
2

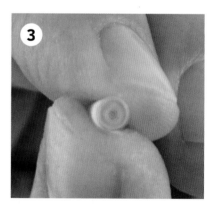
3

Begin by folding over the tip of the end of a paper strip as shown here.

Now roll the strip using your thumb and index finger. Keep the coil straight by pushing gently on it from both sides with your other hand.

When you finish rolling the paper, you should have a coil that looks like the one shown here.

FINISHING A BASIC COIL

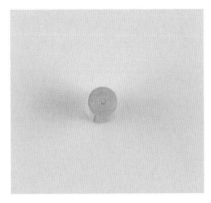

After rolling a paper strip into a coil, let it expand by loosening it slightly, then glue down the end of the paper.

FINISHING A TIGHT COIL

Make a coil, then without letting it expand, apply a thin layer of glue to the end of the paper strip to tightly seal it.

U SHAPE

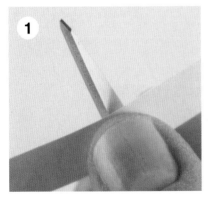

Take a strip and run the blade's edge of a pair of scissors about halfway along to curve it on one side.

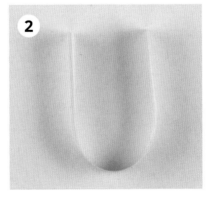

Continue curving the other side until you create a U shape.

ASYMMETRIC U SHAPE

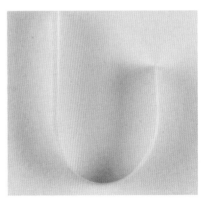

Cut one end of a U shape shorter to create an asymmetric U shape.

C SHAPE

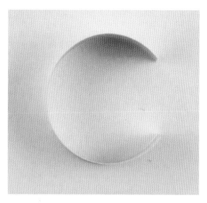

Run the blade's edge of a pair of scissors all the way along one side of a paper strip to curve it into a C. To make a curve in a paper strip that has straight ends, similar to a U shape, start partway along the strip and finish before you get to the end.

V SHAPE

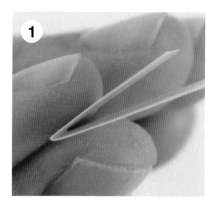

Fold and make a crease on a paper strip at the desired point.

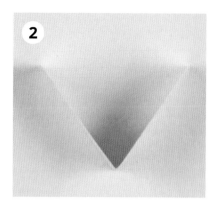

Cut the longer side to make the two sides even.

ASYMMETRIC V SHAPE

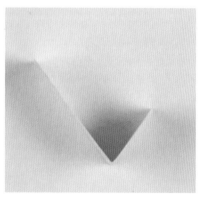

Make a V shape, but cut one side to the desired length to create an asymmetric V shape (with two sides of different lengths).

WAVE SHAPE

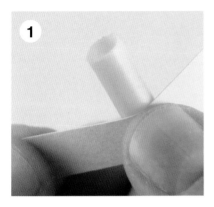

1

Starting near the end of a paper strip, pass a pen top or pen along the paper to make a gentle curve on one side of the strip.

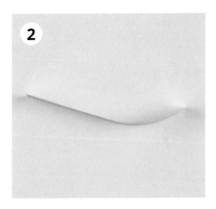

2

You should have a strip with a single gentle curve.

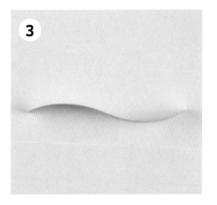

3

Now, gently curve the other end of the strip in the opposite direction to make a wave shape with two similar curves.

ASYMMETRIC WAVE SHAPE

This is similar to the wave shape, but apply less pressure to only slightly curve the second end in the opposite direction, creating uneven curves.

CONTINUOUS WAVE SHAPE

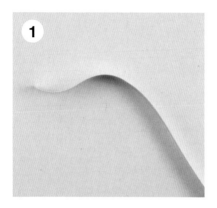

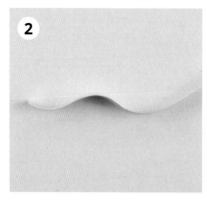

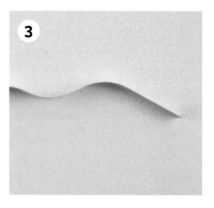

Similar to a wave shape (see page 13) but with more waves along the length of the strip. To start the first wave shape, make a curve for the left section of the wave on the end of the paper.

Then curve the right section of the wave using the pen.

Now, curve the left section of the next wave using the pen.

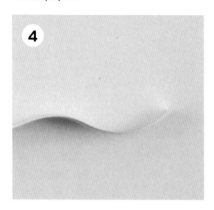

Curve the right section of the wave using the pen. Continue in this way to make as many waves as needed.

DROP SHAPE

Make a U shape (see page 11). Apply a thin layer of glue to on end of the strip. Stick both sides together using a pair of tweezers to hold them, then leave to dry.

You now have a drop shape.

BENT DROP SHAPE

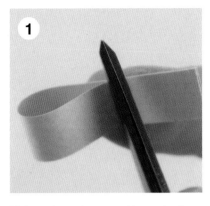

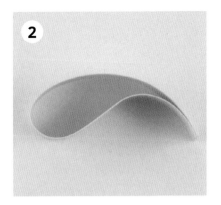

Make a drop shape and leave to dry. Holding the end of the shape, run the blade's edge of a pair of scissors about halfway along to the end.

You now have a bent drop shape.

TEARDROP SHAPE

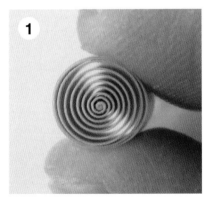

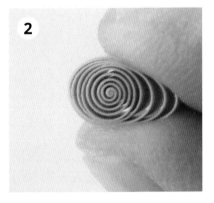

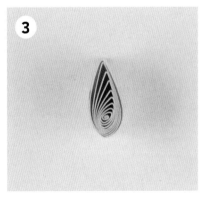

Make a coil (see page 10) and press two sides together along one half of it.

Glue the end of the paper strip in place.

You now have a teardrop shape.

ZIGZAG SHAPE

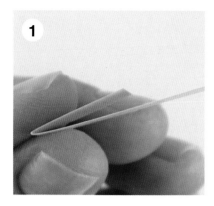

1

Fold and crease the end of a strip of paper at the desired point.

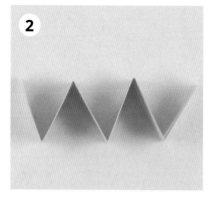

2

Continue making folds in the same way along the length of paper. When you have finished making the folds, trim the end of the strip with a pair of scissors.

ASYMMETRIC ZIGZAG SHAPE

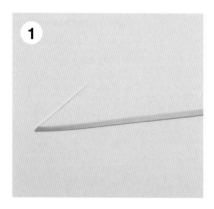

1

Fold and crease the end of a strip of paper at the desired point like a V shape (see page 12).

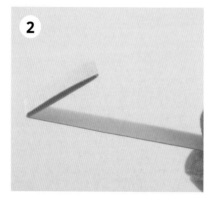

2

Fold the short end in towards the long one.

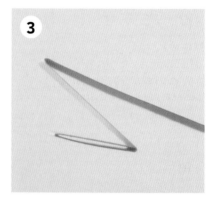

3

Then make a fold in the long section at the desired point.

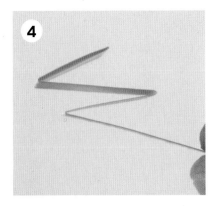

4 To make additional folds, rotate the strip after each fold to make it easier to work with.

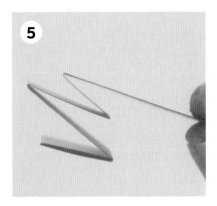

5 Each new fold should create a section that is of a different size than the section before it.

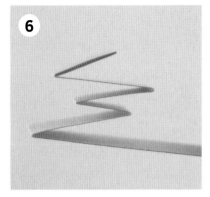

6 As you choose where to make each new fold, compare the folds overall to ensure they are staggered.

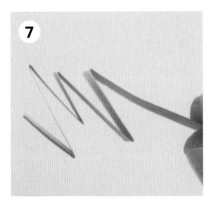

7 Repeat making folds along the strip until you reach the end, making sure the last fold isn't too short.

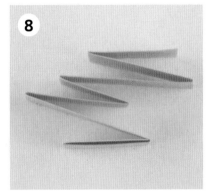

8 You now have an asymmetric zigzag shape.

9 You can apply glue to some of the edges on one end if you want to condense only part of the shape.

10 You can apply glue to all the edges at the end of one side if you want a fanned shape.

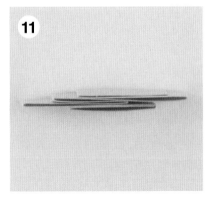

11 If you want a compact shape, apply glue to all the edges.

TIP
Do not try to get the exact shape as it should be folded randomly.

ALMOND SHAPE

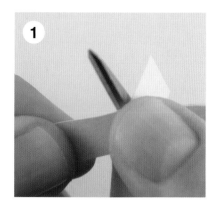

Start by making a V shape in the middle of a paper strip, using the blade's edge of a pair of scissors to mark the fold.

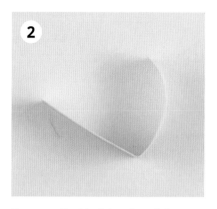

Now, run the blade's edge of the scissors inside the V shape, from the fold to the end of the strip, to curve it towards the inside. Repeat for the opposite side.

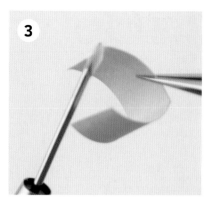

Apply a thin layer of glue to one end of the strip.

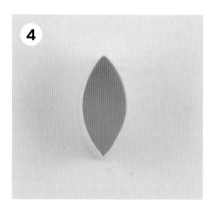

Fix it to the other side of it, using your fingers to hold the ends together. You will now have an almond shape.

CRIMPED SHAPE

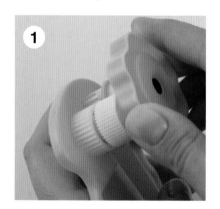

Using the crimper tool, place the paper in the tool and turn it.

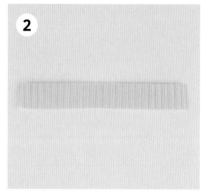

Once you have finished, you should have a shape that looks like this.

Getting started

If you're new to quilling, follow these tips to get to grips with the projects.

• Measure the paper against the template to ascertain the length for cutting it and follow the template to shape and place it.

• For shaping, run the paper against the scissor blade's edge to create a bend or curve, and the more pressure you apply, the greater the bend or curve will be (see also U and C shapes, pages 11 and 12).

• Test each piece in place before applying glue. Make sure it fits and that you have the correct orientation; also, double check which side to apply glue to so that the correct side is glued down.

• Hold the shape with a pair of tweezers. Apply a thin layer of white, clear-drying glue to the bottom of the shape and along the edge of the paper. Using the tweezers, place the shape into your outline and press down lightly with your fingers to secure. Leave to dry.

• The directions in the steps are based on the orientation of the flower in the photograph, so if the flower is turned when working, take care to avoid confusing the left and right sides of a petal or leaf.

USING THE TEMPLATES

To make the tracing, you'll need a blank sheet of 90lb (250gsm) cardstock paper, quilling needle or compass and some sticky tape.

Place the template on top of the cardstock paper. Secure the template with a piece of sticky tape to hold it in place while you're tracing the design.

Take a quilling needle or compass and use it to trace around the outlines. Remove the template. You should be able to see the tracing on the base paper.

Carnation

As a popular birth flower for January, the pink carnation flower symbolizes gratitude and the concept of never forgetting someone. To show the beauty and simplicity of the blossom, one shade of pink has been used for the petals.

materials

- Template on page 163

- Blank sheet of 90lb (250gsm) cardstock

- 11 × ⅜in (28 × 1cm) green cardstock × 2

- 11 × ⅜in (28 × 1cm) pink paper × 4

- 11 × ⅜in (28 × 1cm) forest green paper × 1

- 11 × ⅜in (28 × 1cm) apple green cardstock × 1

- 11 × ⅜in (28 × 1cm) emerald green paper × 1

- 11 × ⅜in (28 × 1cm) light green paper × 1

tools

- Quilling needle or compass

- Scissors

- Tweezers

- White glue

1

To create your base, place a sheet of blank cardstock under the template, then trace the outline and lines onto it using a quilling needle or compass.

2

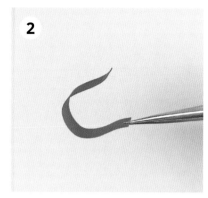

Using green cardstock, make a U shape (see page 11) and slightly bend the tips outward.

3

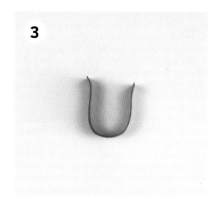

Apply a thin layer of glue along one edge of the card and place it about centre of the base, to start making the flower's green 'receptacle'.

4

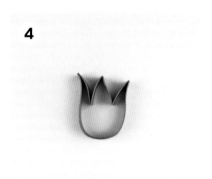

Make an asymmetrical zigzag shape (see pages 16–17) from green cardstock. Apply a thin layer of glue; place it to form the top of the flower's receptacle.

5

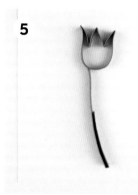

Using green cardstock, make a stalk, folding up the bottom end to create a double layer in the lower half. Apply a thin layer of glue and place it below the receptacle.

6

Using green cardstock, make the leaf, following a bent drop shape (see page 15). Apply a thin layer of glue and place it on the right side of the stalk, above the double layer.

7

Make a curved shape for the top right of the stalk, using green cardstock. Apply a thin layer of glue and place it above the leaf.

8

Using green cardstock, make the second leaf. Apply a thin layer of glue and place it as shown on the left side of the stalk.

9

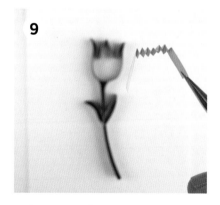

Make a shape from pink paper that has two long straight ends and tiny zigzags (see page 16) in the middle (the zigzags do not need to be even or the same as shown above).

10

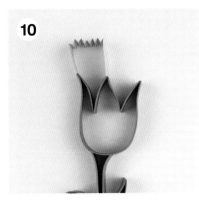

Apply a thin layer of glue and place the first petal on the left side above the receptacle, as shown above.

11

Using pink paper, make an L shape that will be straight down one side and zigzag on top. Apply a thin layer of glue and place it inside the petal.

12

Make another shape similar to the one in the previous step using pink paper. Apply a thin layer of glue and place it on the right of the petal.

13

Make a shape similar to the one in the previous step using pink paper. Apply a thin layer of glue and place it on the right side of the petals.

14

Make a zigzag shape using pink paper. Apply a thin layer of glue and place it at the top right side of the petals.

15

Using pink paper, make one part of the strip into zigzags. Bend the strip between them and the straight end, apply a thin layer of glue and place it on the right side of the petals.

16

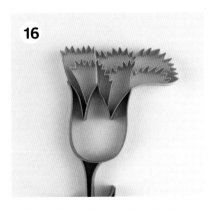

Make a zigzag shape using pink paper, apply a thin layer of glue and place it horizontally inside the previous petal.

17

Make a shape from pink paper with straight ends and zigzags in the middle. Bend the straight ends as shown above, apply a thin layer of glue and place it on the right side.

18

Using pink paper, make a shape with a straight end and zigzag end. Bend the straight part slightly as shown above, apply a thin layer of glue and place it on the left side of the petals.

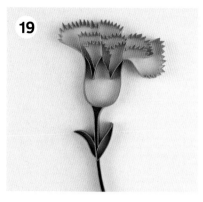

19

Make a shape from pink paper straight on both sides and zigzags in the middle. Apply a thin layer of glue and place it at the top, to the right of the previous petal shape.

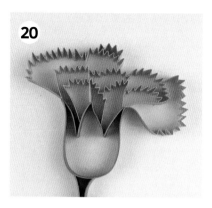

20

Make a mini zigzag shape using pink paper, apply a thin layer of glue and place it above the previous petal.

21

Make a mini zigzag a bit longer than the previous step using pink paper, apply a thin layer of glue and place it on the left side of the previous petal.

22

Using pink paper, make a shape that is straight on one side and zigzag shape on the other, apply a thin layer of glue and place it on the left side of the petals.

23

Make a shape from pink paper with two short straight ends and small zigzags in the middle, apply a thin layer of glue and place it on the top right of the petals.

24

From pink paper, make a shape like the previous one but shorter. Apply a thin layer of glue and place it on the right side of the previous petal.

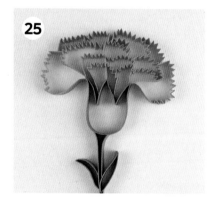

25

Make a mini zigzag shape using pink paper, apply a thin layer of glue and place it on the left side of the previous petal.

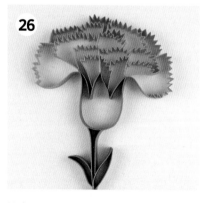

26

Make a mini zigzag shape using pink paper, apply a thin layer of glue and place it on top, towards the centre.

27

Using pink paper, make a shorter mini zigzag shape, apply a thin layer of glue and place it on top, to the left of the previous petal.

28

Using green cardstock, make a pair of sepals from almond shapes (see page 18). Apply a thin layer of glue and place them inside the bottom section of the receptacle.

29

Fill the two sepals: make compact zigzag shapes from the forest green paper strip, apply glue and place them inside.

30

Make a wave shape (see page 13) from green cardstock, apply a thin layer of glue and place it vertically in the centre of the receptacle.

31

Make two more wave shapes from the green cardstock. Apply a thin layer of glue and place them to the left and right of the step 30 piece.

32

Make a slightly bent shape using green cardstock, apply a thin layer of glue and place it in the far left side inside the receptacle.

33

Using the apple green cardstock, make a wave shape and a slightly bent shape. Apply a thin layer of glue and place them inside the leaves.

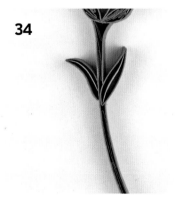

34

Fill the stalk with zigzag shapes using emerald green paper.

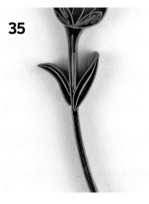

35

Finally, make a zigzag shape using light green paper, apply a thin layer of glue and place it in the upper half of the stalk.

Pansy

The birth flower of February is the pansy, and purple is the most common pansy flower colour. They are both symbols of love, compassion and thoughtfulness.

materials

- Template on page 162

- Blank sheet of 90lb (250gsm) cardstock

- 11 × ⅜in (28 × 1cm) sun yellow paper × 1

- 11 × ⅜in (28 × 1cm) light yellow paper × 1

- 11 × ⅜in (28 × 1cm) lilac cardstock × 4

- 11 × ⅜in (28 × 1cm) purple paper × 1

- 11 × ⅜in (28 × 1cm) forest green cardstock × 1

tools

- Quilling needle or compass

- Scissors

- Tweezers

- White glue

1

To create your base, place a sheet of blank cardstock under the template, then trace the outline and lines onto it using a quilling needle or compass.

2

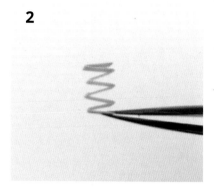

Make a zigzag shape (see page 16) using a strip of sun yellow paper.

3

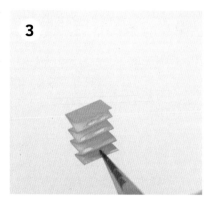

On one side only of the zigzags, apply a thin layer of glue along one edge of each point.

4

Stick the wings together as shown above.

5

Apply a thin layer of glue and place the fanned strip on the base paper.

6

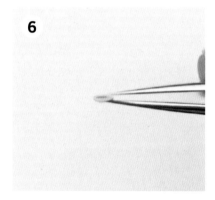

Make two mini oval shapes as shown above using light yellow paper.

7

Apply a thin layer of glue and place the two shapes on the left and right sides of the step 5 shape.

8

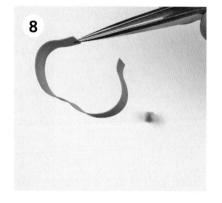

Make a curved shape as shown above, making a wave shape (see page 13) in the middle and C-like shapes (see page 12) on each end, using lilac cardstock.

9

Apply a thin layer of glue and place it with the ends on each side of the other pieces and curved below them, as shown above.

10

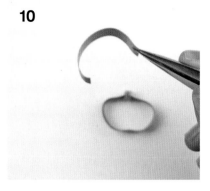

Make a C shape, as shown above, using lilac cardstock.

11

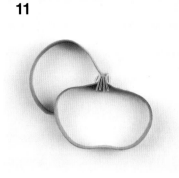

Apply a thin layer of glue and place it to the top left of the previous petal.

12

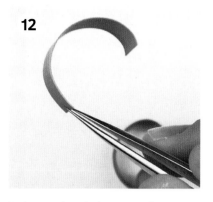

Make another C shape, as shown above, using lilac cardstock.

13

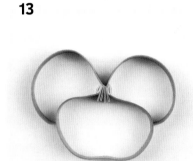

Apply a thin layer of glue and place it to the top right of the previous petals.

14

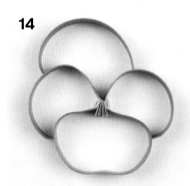

Make a similar C shape using lilac cardstock, apply a thin layer of glue and place it above the previously placed petals.

15

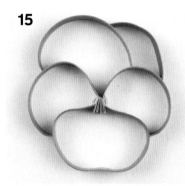

Slightly bend a piece of lilac cardstock, apply a thin layer of glue and place it to the right side of the previous petal.

16

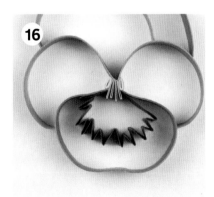

Make a zigzag shape using the purple paper, apply a thin layer of glue and place it inside the bottom petal, as shown above.

17

Make another zigzag shape using the purple paper, apply a thin layer of glue and place it inside the left-hand petal, as shown above.

18

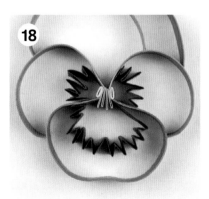

Make another zigzag shape using the purple paper, apply a thin layer of glue and place it inside the right-hand petal, as shown above.

19

Cut six short pieces of purple paper, apply a thin layer of glue and place them from the zigzags of the bottom petal to the centre, as shown above.

20

Slightly bend three short pieces of lilac cardstock. Apply a thin layer of glue and place them from the zigzags to the bottom of the petal.

21

Slightly bend three short pieces of lilac cardstock. Apply a thin layer of glue and place them alongside the step 20 pieces.

22

Slightly bend three short pieces of lilac cardstock. Apply a thin layer of glue and place them to the right of the step 21 pieces.

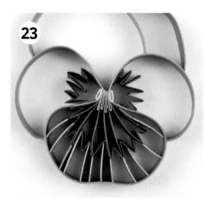

23

Slightly bend three short pieces of lilac cardstock. Apply a thin layer of glue and place them to the right of the step 22 pieces. The first petal is now finished.

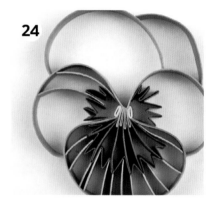

24

Slightly bend two short pieces of lilac cardstock. Apply a thin layer of glue and place them inside the top of the left-hand petal.

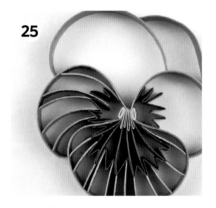

25

Slightly bend three short pieces of lilac cardstock. Apply a thin layer of glue and place them below the step 24 pieces.

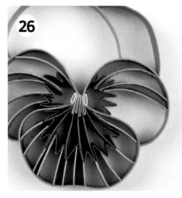

26

Slightly bend three short pieces of lilac cardstock. Apply a thin layer of glue; place them inside the top of the right-hand petal.

27

Slightly bend two short pieces of lilac cardstock. Apply a thin layer of glue and place them below the step 26 pieces.

28

Cut two strips of lilac cardstock, bend them slightly and cut one end so it is round, as shown above.

29

Apply a thin layer of glue and place each one close together in the top petal, as shown above.

30

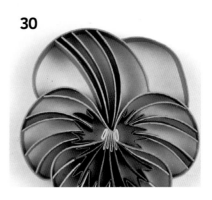

Cut three strips of lilac cardstock, bend them slightly and round off one end. Apply a thin layer of glue and place them on the left of the step 29 pieces.

31

Cut two shorter strips of lilac cardstock, bend them slightly and round off one end. Apply a thin layer of glue and place them on the left of the step 30 pieces.

32

Cut one strip of lilac cardstock, bend it slightly and cut one end round. Apply a thin layer of glue and place it on the right of the step 29 pieces.

33

Slightly bend three short pieces of lilac cardstock. Apply a thin layer of glue and place them inside the right half of the last petal.

34

Slightly bend two short pieces of lilac cardstock. Apply a thin layer of glue and place them inside the left half of the last petal.

35

Cut and slightly bend one strip of forest green cardstock. Apply a thin layer of glue and place it as the centre part of the leaf on the left side of the flower.

36

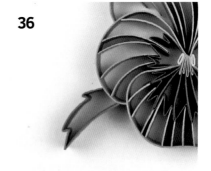

Using forest green cardstock, make an asymmetric zigzag shape (see pages 16–17) similar to above, apply a thin layer of glue and place it above the step 35 shape.

37

Make an asymmetrical shape like above from forest green cardstock, apply a thin layer of glue and place it below the step 35 shape to finish the leaf.

38

Cut one strip of forest green cardstock and slightly bend it. Apply a thin layer of glue and place it to the right of the previously made leaf.

39

For the left side of the bigger leaf, make an asymmetrical zigzag-like shape from forest green cardstock as shown above and place it to the left side of the step 38 piece.

40

For the right side of the bigger leaf, make an asymmetrical zigzag-like shape from forest green cardstock as shown above and place it on the right side of the step 38 piece.

41

Cut two short strips of forest green cardstock and slightly bend them. Apply a thin layer of glue and place them inside the left side of the smaller leaf, as shown above.

42

Cut two short strips of forest green cardstock and slightly bend them. Apply a thin layer of glue and place them inside the right side of the smaller leaf.

43

Cut two short strips of forest green cardstock and slightly bend them. Apply a thin layer of glue and place them inside the left side of the bigger leaf.

44

Finally, cut two short strips of forest green cardstock and slightly bend them. Apply a thin layer of glue and place them inside the right side of the bigger leaf.

Daffodil

With cheerful yellow blossoms, daffodils are symbols of spring, new beginnings and rebirth. They are March's birth flower, and they are among the first flowers to emerge from the soil after winter.

materials

• Template on page 162

• Blank sheet of 90lb (250gsm) cardstock

• 11 × ⅜in (28 × 1cm) sun yellow paper × 1

• 11 × ⅜in (28 × 1cm) yellow paper × 2

• 11 × ⅜in (28 × 1cm) forest green cardstock × 2

tools

• Quilling needle or compass

• Scissors

• Tweezers

• White glue

1

To create your base, place a sheet of blank cardstock under the template, then trace the outline and lines onto it using a quilling needle or compass.

2

Start with the trumpet part. Make a U shape (see page 11) from the sun yellow paper, bend the ends outwards. Apply a thin layer of glue and place it on the base as shown.

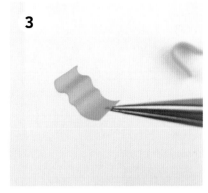

3

Using the sun yellow paper, make a continuous asymmetric wave shape (see pages 13 and 14) like the one shown above.

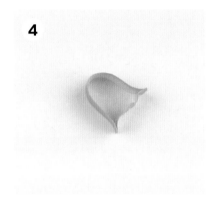

4

Apply a thin layer of glue and place it just inside the top end of the trumpet.

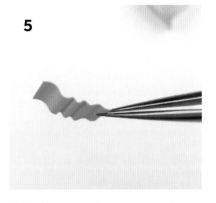

5

Using the sun yellow paper, make a slightly longer but similar shape to the step 3 shape.

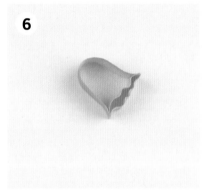

6

Apply a thin layer of glue and place it at the end of the trumpet, to the right of the previous piece.

7

Curl one end of a piece of sun yellow paper.

8

Apply a thin layer of glue and place it inside the trumpet, alongside the top edge.

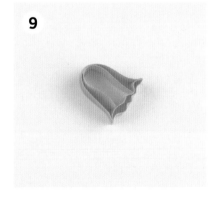

9

Make an asymmetric wave shape using sun yellow paper, apply a thin layer of glue and place it inside the trumpet, alongside the bottom edge.

10

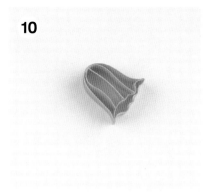

Cut a piece from the sun yellow paper and bend it slightly. Apply a thin layer of glue and place it in the centre of the trumpet.

11

Make an asymmetric wave shape using the sun yellow paper, apply a thin layer of glue and place it on the left of the step 10 piece.

12

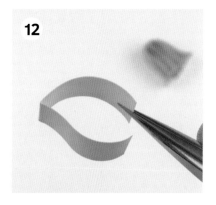

Using yellow paper, make an almond shape (see page 18), with a wave on one side, as shown above.

13

Apply a thin layer of glue and place the first petal to the right and above the trumpet.

14

Repeat step 12 to make a similar shape using the yellow paper. Apply a thin layer of glue and place the second petal on the left side.

15

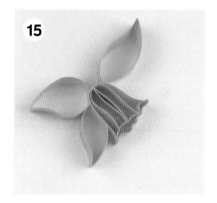

Make another almond-like shape from the yellow paper, following the template. Apply a thin layer of glue and place the third petal at the bottom, to the left of the trumpet.

16

Again, make an almond-like shape from the yellow paper using the template. Apply a thin layer of glue and place the fourth petal between the previous two.

17

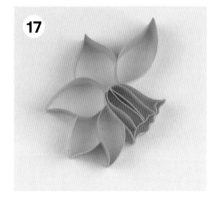

Make an almond-like shape from the yellow paper using the template. Apply a thin layer of glue and place the fifth petal between the first and second petals in steps 13 and 14.

18

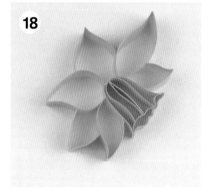

Make an almond-like shape from the yellow paper using the template. Apply a thin layer of glue and place the sixth petal to the right of the second step 14 petal.

19

Slightly bend a piece of yellow paper, apply a thin layer of glue and place it inside the step 18 petal.

20

Make an asymmetric wave shape using the yellow paper. Apply a thin layer of glue and place it inside the next petal on the left.

21

Slightly bend a piece of yellow paper, apply a thin layer of glue and place it inside the next petal on the left.

22

Make an asymmetric wave shape using the yellow paper. Apply a thin layer of glue and place it inside the next petal on the left.

23

Slightly bend a piece of yellow paper, apply a thin layer of glue and place it inside the next petal on the left.

24

Make an asymmetric wave shape using the yellow paper. Apply a thin layer of glue and place it inside the next petal on the left.

25

Next, make the leaf on the right. Slightly bend a piece of forest green cardstock and shape it as shown.

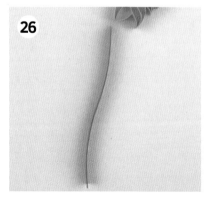

26

Apply a thin layer of glue and place it just below the blossom, at the lowest left-hand point, as shown.

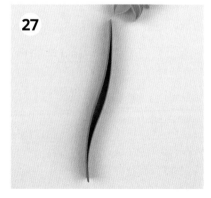

27

Using forest green cardstock, make a shape similar to the step 25 piece, slightly more curved. Apply a thin layer of glue and place it along the right side of the previous piece.

28

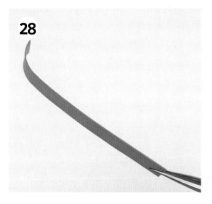

For the stalk, make a shape with a slight curve at one end, using the forest green cardstock.

29

Apply a thin layer of glue and place it with the curve going into the flowerhead and the bottom end connected to the leaf.

30

Make a similar shape to the step 28 piece, using forest green cardstock. Apply a thin layer of glue and place it to form the left side of the stalk.

31

Slightly bend a piece of the forest green cardstock as shown above. Apply a thin layer of glue and place on the left of stalk, with the bottom ends meeting.

32

Make a shape similar to the step 31 piece, but slightly more curved, from forest green cardstock. Apply a thin layer of glue and place along the left side of the step 31 piece.

33

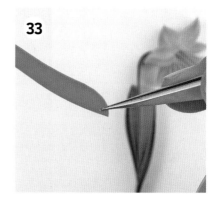

To fill the right-hand leaf, prepare a slightly bent piece and trim both ends so they are rounded.

34

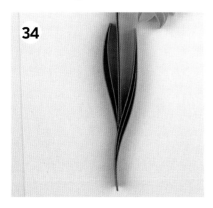

Apply a thin layer of glue and place it inside the leaf on the right.

35

Repeat steps 33 and 34 to fill the inside of the left-hand leaf. The flower is now complete.

Daisy

April's birth flower, the daisy, symbolizes purity, innocence and true love. They are often used in wedding bouquets as well as bouquets for newborns, and the petals that encircle their yellow centres range in colour from white to pink.

materials

- Template on page 165
- Blank sheet of 90lb (250gsm) cardstock
- 11 × ⅜in (28 × 1cm) yellow paper × 3
- 11 × ⅜in (28 × 1cm) amber paper × 2
- 11 × ⅜in (28 × 1cm) white paper × 5

tools

- Quilling needle or compass
- Scissors
- Quilling tool (optional)
- Tweezers
- White glue

To create your base, place a sheet of blank cardstock under the template; trace the outline and lines onto it using a needle or compass. Copy over the circles and numbers.

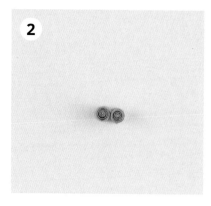

Make two coils using 1¾in (4.5cm)-long pieces of yellow paper. Apply a thin layer of glue; place them on the circles with the number 1.

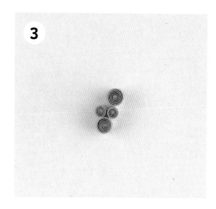

Make two coils using 3in (8cm)-long pieces of amber paper. Apply a thin layer of glue and place them on the circles with the number 2.

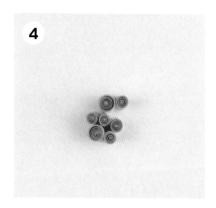

Make three coils using 2in (5cm)-long pieces of yellow paper. Apply a thin layer of glue and place them on the circles with the number 3.

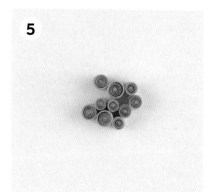

Make three coils using 2⅛in (5.5cm)-long pieces of amber paper. Apply a thin layer of glue and place them on the circles with the number 4.

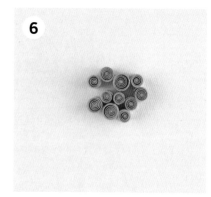

Make one coil using a 1¾in (4.5cm)-long piece of yellow paper. Apply a thin layer of glue and place it on the circle with the number 5.

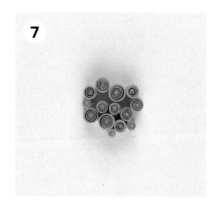

Make three coils using 1⅜in (3.5cm)-long pieces of amber paper. Apply a thin layer of glue; place them on the circles with the number 6.

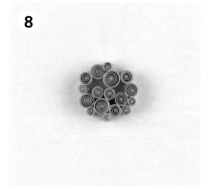

Make three coils using 1in (2.5cm)-long pieces of yellow paper. Apply a thin layer of glue and place them on the circles with the number 7.

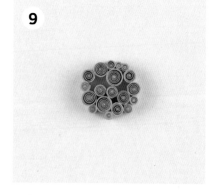

Make two coils using ¾in (2cm)-long pieces of amber paper. Apply a thin layer of glue and place them on the circles with the number 8.

10

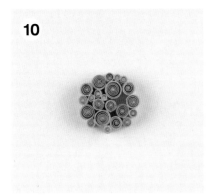

Make three coils using ¾in (2cm)-long pieces of yellow paper. Apply a thin layer of glue and place them on the circles with the number 9.

11

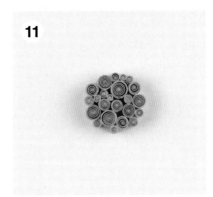

Make one coil using an 1⅛in (3cm)-long piece of yellow paper. Apply a thin layer of glue and place it on the circle with the number 10.

12

Make a U shape (see page 11) from a piece of white paper and slightly bend one end. Apply a thin layer of glue and place it above the circles.

13

Cut a piece of white paper and bend one end. Apply a thin layer of glue and place it on the right side of the previous step 12 piece. You now have a full petal.

14

Work clockwise for the remaining petals. Make a U shape from white paper, apply a thin layer of glue and place it to the right of the first petal, leaving a slight gap.

15

Cut a piece of white paper and bend it slightly. Apply a thin layer of glue and place it inside the previous shape to finish the second petal.

16

Make an asymmetric U shape (see page 11) using white paper. Apply a thin layer of glue and place it in the gap between the two petals.

17

Cut a piece of white paper and bend one end. Apply a thin layer of glue and place it on the right side of the step 16 piece to finish the petal.

18

Make an asymmetric U shape using white paper. Apply a thin layer of glue and place it on the right side of the step 15 petal.

19

Cut a piece of white paper and slightly bend. Apply a thin layer of glue and place it inside the previously made petal.

20

Make a U shape using white paper. Apply a thin layer of glue and place it below the previously made petal, leaving a slight gap.

21

Cut a piece of white paper and slightly bend one end. Apply a thin layer of glue and place it above the previously placed U shape.

22

Cut a piece of white paper and slightly bend. Apply a thin layer of glue and place it inside the step 20 U-shape piece.

23

Make an asymmetric U shape using white paper. Apply a thin layer of glue and place it below the previously made petal.

24

Cut a piece of white paper and slightly bend one end. Apply a thin layer of glue and place it below the previously made U-shape piece.

25

Make a U shape using white paper. Apply a thin layer of glue and place it below the previously made petal, leaving a slight gap.

26

Cut a piece of white paper and slightly bend one end. Apply a thin layer of glue and place it inside the previously made U-shape piece.

27

Make an asymmetric U shape using white paper. Apply a thin layer of glue and place it between the last two petals made in steps 23–26.

28

Cut a piece of white paper and slightly bend one end. Apply a thin layer of glue and place it just below the previous step 27 piece.

29

Make a U shape using white paper. Apply a thin layer of glue and place to the left of the step 26 petal, leaving a slight gap.

30

Cut a piece of white paper and slightly bend it. Apply a thin layer of glue and place it inside the U shape made in step 29.

31

Make a U shape using white paper. Apply a thin layer of glue and place between the last two previously made petals.

32

Cut a piece of white paper and slightly bend it. Apply a thin layer of glue and place it inside the U shape made in step 31.

33

Make a U shape using white paper. Slightly bend one side, apply a thin layer of glue and place it on the left side of the previously made petal.

34

Cut a piece of white paper and slightly bend one end. Apply a thin layer of glue and place it on the right side of the previously made U-shape piece.

35

Make an asymmetric U shape using white paper. Apply a thin layer of glue and place it between the last two previously made petals.

36

Cut a piece of white paper and slightly bend one end. Apply a thin layer of glue and place on the left side of the previously made piece.

37

Make an asymmetric U shape using white paper. Apply a thin layer of glue and place on the left side of the step 34 piece.

38

Cut a piece of white paper and slightly bend. Apply a thin layer of glue and place it inside the previously made petal.

39

Make a U shape using white paper. Apply a thin layer of glue and place it above the previously made petal, leaving a slight gap.

40

Cut a piece of white paper and slightly bend one end. Apply a thin layer of glue and place it on the right side of the previously made shape.

41

Make a U shape using white paper. Slightly bend one side, apply a thin layer of glue and place it above the previously made petal.

42

Cut a piece of white paper and slightly bend one end. Apply a thin layer of glue and place it above the previously made U shape piece.

43

Make an asymmetric U shape using white paper. Apply a thin layer of glue and place it between the two previously made petals.

44

Cut a piece of white paper and slightly bend. Apply a thin layer of glue and place it inside the step 43 U shape piece.

45

Make a U shape using white paper. Apply a thin layer of glue and place it above the step 42 petal.

46

Cut a piece of white paper and slightly bend. Apply a thin layer of glue and place it inside the previously made U shape piece.

47

Make an asymmetric U shape using white paper. Apply a thin layer of glue and place it between the two previously made petals.

48

Cut a piece of white paper and slightly bend one end. Apply a thin layer of glue and place it above the step 47 U shape piece.

49

Make an asymmetric U shape using white paper. Apply a thin layer of glue and place it above the step 46 petal, with one end on the side of the neighbouring petal.

50

Cut a piece of white paper and slightly bend. Apply a thin layer of glue and place it inside the previously made U-shape piece.

51

Make a U shape using white paper. Apply a thin layer of glue and place it in the gap between the first petal and the previously made petal, leaving a slight gap on the left.

52

Cut a piece of white paper and slightly bend one end. Apply a thin layer of glue and place it on the left side of the previously made U shape.

53

Make an asymmetric U shape using white paper. Apply a thin layer of glue and place it between the first petal and the previously made petal.

54

Finally, cut a piece of white paper and slightly bend. Apply a thin layer of glue and place it on the left side of the previously made U-shape piece.

Lily of the valley

With its small white bells, the lily of the valley – the birth flower of May – signifies purity, youth, sincerity and happiness. It is a popular choice for all kinds of celebrations.

materials

• Template on page 164

• Blank sheet of 90lb (250gsm) cardstock

• 11 × ⅜in (28 × 1cm) white paper × 2

• 11 × ⅜in (28 × 1cm) forest green cardstock × 4

• 11 × ⅜in (28 × 1cm) emerald green paper × 2

tools

• Quilling needle or compass

• Scissors

• Tweezers

• Quilling crimping tool

• White glue

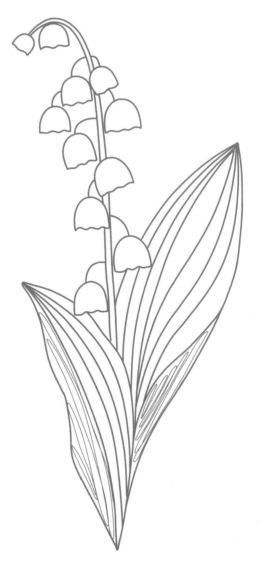

1

To create your base, place a sheet of blank cardstock under the template, then trace the outline and lines onto it using a quilling needle or compass.

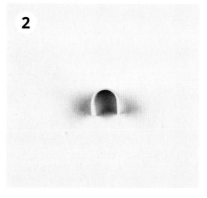

2

Make a U shape (see page 11) using a piece of white paper. Apply a thin layer of glue and place on the marks for the bottom left bell flower.

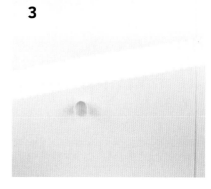

3

Cut a 6in (15cm)-long piece of white paper and pass it through a quilling crimper tool.

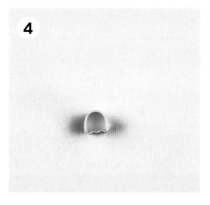

4

Cut a small piece from the crimped paper, apply a thin layer of glue and place it between the ends of the U shape, forming the first bell flower.

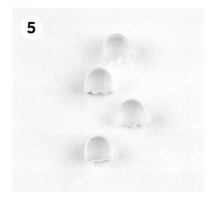

5

Repeat steps 2 and 4 to make three more bell-shaped flowers.

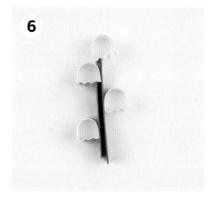

6

Make the stalk using forest green cardstock, folding it to make two sides, as shown above. Apply a thin layer of glue and carefully place it between the bells.

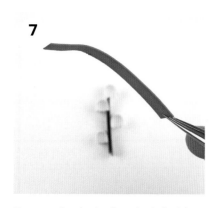

7

Next, make the leaf on the left side. Using forest green cardstock, make a slightly bent shape.

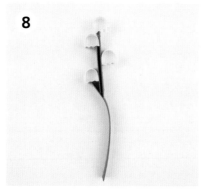

8

Apply a thin layer of glue and place it with the top curved end starting at the lowest flower on the left side.

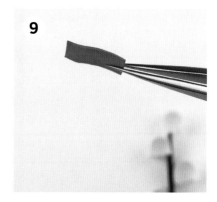

9

Make the tip of the leaf to continue it beyond the flower. Using forest green cardstock, make a slight wave shape (see page 13).

10

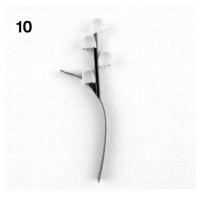

Apply a thin layer of glue and place it on the left side of the bottom bell flower, continuing the line of the leaf.

11

Slightly bend a piece of forest green cardstock, apply a thin layer of glue and place it between the previously placed step 8 and 10 leaf pieces.

12

Make a continuous wave shape (see page 14) using forest green cardstock. Apply a thin layer of glue and place it on the left of the previously placed piece.

13

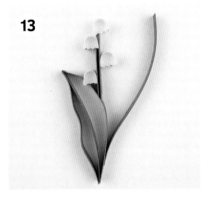

Using forest green cardstock, make a shape with a slight wave. Apply a thin layer of glue and place it starting at the bottom right side of the leaf.

14

Slightly bend a piece of forest green cardstock, apply a thin layer of glue and place it from the top of the previously placed piece, ending at the lower right-hand bell flower.

15

Slightly bend a shorter piece of forest green cardstock, apply a thin layer of glue and place it between the bell flower and stalk, continuing the line of the leaf.

16

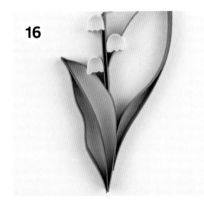

Make an asymmetric wave shape using forest green cardstock, apply a thin layer of glue and place it inside the bottom right side of the right-hand leaf.

17

Slightly bend a piece of forest green cardstock, apply a thin layer of glue and place it vertically, slightly off-centre, in the right-hand leaf.

18

Repeat steps 2 and 4 to make three more flowers from white paper, with one of them smaller. Apply a thin layer of glue; place them above the other bells, the smaller one on top.

19

Make the rest of the stalk, using forest green cardstock and folding it to make two sides; apply a thin layer of glue and place it carefully between the bells.

20

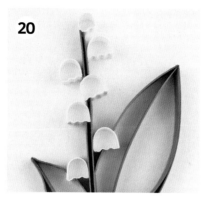

Cut a small piece of forest green cardstock, apply a thin layer of glue and place it on the stalk part between the two flowers.

21

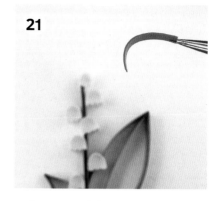

Make a curved shape, as shown above, using forest green cardstock.

22

Apply a thin layer of glue and place it to continue the stalk above the top smaller flower, curving to the left.

23

Again using forest green cardstock, make a shape similar to the one in step 21. Apply a thin layer of glue and place it on the left side of the previously placed shape.

24

Repeat steps 2 and 4 to make four more flowers using white paper, with one of them smaller. Apply a thin layer of glue and place them as shown above.

25

Cut two small pieces from forest green cardstock; bend them slightly. Apply a thin layer of glue and place them between the stalk and the two flowers third and fourth from top.

26

Cut six more small pieces from forest green cardstock and bend them slightly. Apply a thin layer of glue and place them between the stalk and lower flowers.

27

Make an asymmetric zigzag shape (see pages 16–17) using emerald green paper. Apply a thin layer of glue and place it in the left-hand part of the leaf on the left side.

28

Slightly bend a piece of forest green cardstock, apply a thin layer of glue and place it inside the top right edge of the left-hand leaf.

29

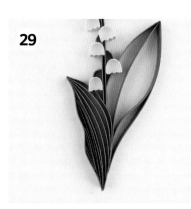

Slightly bend two pieces of forest green cardstock, apply a thin layer of glue and place them inside the right side of the left-hand leaf.

30

Make an asymmetric zigzag shape using emerald green paper, apply a thin layer of glue and place it inside the right-hand leaf in the bottom right section.

31

Make an asymmetric wave shape (page 13) using forest green cardstock, apply a thin layer of glue and place it inside the right-hand leaf along the right edge.

32

Make an asymmetric wave shape using forest green cardstock, apply a thin layer of glue and place it to the left of the previously placed piece.

33

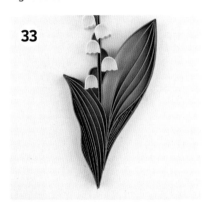

Make an asymmetric wave shape using forest green cardstock, apply a thin layer of glue and place it to the left of the previously placed piece.

34

Slightly bend a piece of forest green cardstock, apply a thin layer of glue and place it in the left-hand section of the right-hand leaf.

35

Slightly bend a piece of forest green cardstock, apply a thin layer of glue and place it to the left of the previous piece, above the bell flower.

36

Finally, slightly bend a piece of forest green cardstock. Apply a thin layer of glue and place it to the left of the previous piece, below the bell flower.

Honeysuckle

June's birth flower, honeysuckle conveys messages of sweetness and affection. It is believed that the honeysuckle can bring both good luck and good fortune to your home.

materials

- Template on page 165
- Blank sheet of 90lb (250gsm) cardstock
- 11 × ⅜in (28 × 1cm) green paper × 2
- 11 × ⅜in (28 × 1cm) pink paper × 2
- 11 × ⅜in (28 × 1cm) salmon pink paper × 1
- 11 × ⅜in (28 × 1cm) light pink paper × 1
- 1⅛ × ⅜in (3 × 1cm) white cardstock × 1
- ⅜ × ⅜in (1 × 1cm) yellow paper × 2

tools

- Quilling needle or compass
- Scissors
- Tweezers
- White glue
- Ruler
- Craft knife
- Cutting mat
- Quilling tool (optional)

1

To create your base, place a sheet of blank cardstock under the template, then trace the outline and lines onto it using a quilling needle or compass.

2

Make a U shape (see page 11) using green paper, apply a thin layer of glue and place it as shown above to start building a green 'receptacle' for the flower's petals.

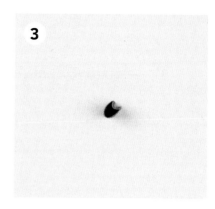

3

Make a C shape (see page 12) using green paper, apply a thin layer of glue and place it on the top of the U shape positioned in step 2.

4

Make a U shape using green paper, apply a thin layer of glue and place it as shown above, projecting to the right from the C shape positioned in step 3.

5

Make another U shape using green paper, apply a thin layer of glue and place it to the right of the U shape positioned in step 4.

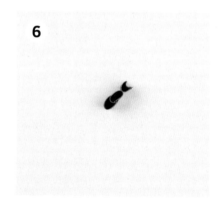

6

Make a C shape using green paper, apply a thin layer of glue and place it on the top of the U shape positioned in step 5.

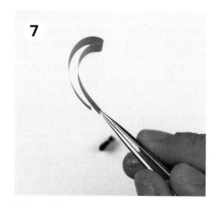

7

Using pink paper, make a bent drop shape (see page 15) like the one shown above.

8

Apply a thin layer of glue and place the two ends starting inside the C shape with the looped part extending to the right.

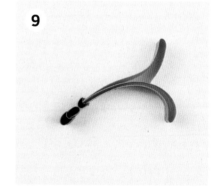

9

Make an asymmetric bent drop shape, using pink paper, to form an upper petal, apply a thin layer of glue and place it extending from the receptacle over the lower petal.

10

Make a shape using salmon pink paper with one end curved, then cut the other end so it is rounded off.

11

Apply a thin layer of glue and place it on the right side of the step 9 petal, with the curved side at the top.

12

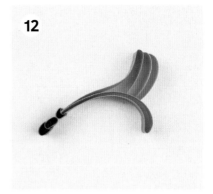

Make a shape similar to the one in step 10 using salmon pink paper. Apply a thin layer of glue and place it on the right side of the shape made in the previous step.

13

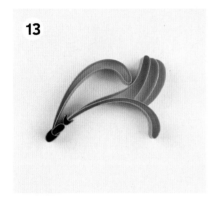

Repeat step 7 using pink paper, apply a thin layer of glue and place it above and left of the previously made petals, ending it slightly more to the left.

14

Repeat step 9 using pink paper, apply a thin layer of glue and place it above and left of the previously placed petal.

15

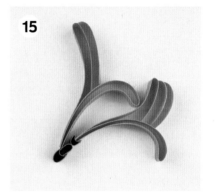

Repeat step 10 using salmon pink paper. Apply a thin layer of glue and place it on the right side of the previously placed shape.

16

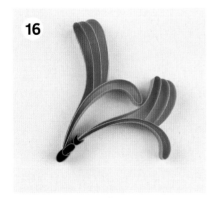

Repeat step 10 using salmon pink paper. Apply a thin layer of glue and place it on the right side of the previously placed shape.

17

Make the shape as shown above, similar to the step 7 shape, using pink paper.

18

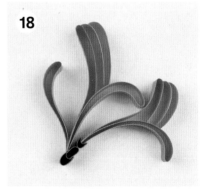

Apply a thin layer of glue and place it on the left side of the other petals, extending from the same end as the step 13 petal.

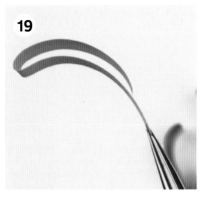

19

Make the shape as shown above, similar to the step 7 shape, using pink paper.

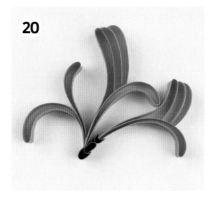

20

Apply a thin layer of glue and place it to the left side of the step 18 shape.

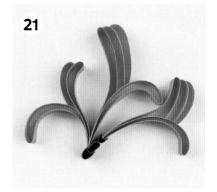

21

Repeat step 10 using salmon pink paper. Apply a thin layer of glue and place it on the left side of the step 18 shape.

22

Repeat step 10 using salmon pink paper. Apply a thin layer of glue and place it to the left side of the previously placed shape.

23

Make a bent drop shape using pink paper. Apply a thin layer of glue and place it below the other petals on the right-hand side.

24

Slightly bend a piece of light pink paper, apply a thin layer of glue and place it inside the shape made in the previous step.

25

Slightly bend a piece of green paper, apply a thin layer of glue and place it as the left side of the stalk.

26

Slightly bend a piece of green paper, apply a thin layer of glue and place it as the right side of the stalk.

27

For the middle part of the leaf, slightly bend green paper. Apply a thin layer of glue and place it extending from the right of the stalk.

28

Make an almond shape (see page 18) using green paper.

29

Apply a thin layer of glue and place it around the previously placed piece.

30

Cut three pieces of green paper and slightly bend them. Apply a thin layer of glue and place them inside the lower half of the leaf.

31

Cut another three pieces of green paper and slightly bend them. Apply a thin layer of glue and place them inside the upper part of the leaf.

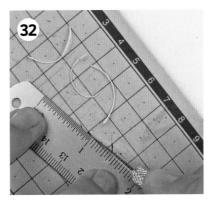

32

Cut white cardstock horizontally into very thin strips, using a craft knife and metal ruler. You will need 18 strips in total.

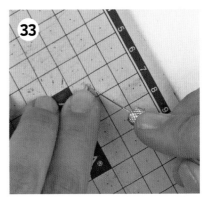

33

Using ⅜in (1cm)-wide yellow paper, make two tight coils (see page 11). Then cut them horizontally to make 18 small pieces.

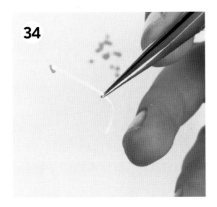

34

Apply a thin layer of glue to each white thin strip and attach one of the small yellow tight coils.

35

Glue six white strips together at the ends without the yellow coils. You will have three sets in total.

36

Finally, apply a thin layer of glue and place them with the glued ends between the petals as shown above.

Water lily

July's birth flower is the water lily. This flower rests on the surface for only about four days before settling under the water. You create one using paper and keep it in your home to bring beauty, hope, wellness and peace.

materials

- Template on page 165
- Blank sheet of 90lb (250gsm) cardstock
- 11 × ⅜in (28 × 1cm) pink paper × 3
- 11 × ⅜in (28 × 1cm) mint paper × 1
- 11 × ⅜in (28 × 1cm) yellow paper × 1
- 11 × ⅜in (28 × 1cm) white paper × 1
- 11 × ⅜in (28 × 1cm) light yellow paper × 1
- 11 × ⅜in (28 × 1cm) light pink paper × 2
- 11 × ⅜in (28 × 1cm) salmon pink paper × 1

tools

- Quilling needle or compass
- Scissors
- Tweezers
- White glue

1

To create your base, place a sheet of blank cardstock under the template, then trace the outline and lines onto it using a quilling needle or compass.

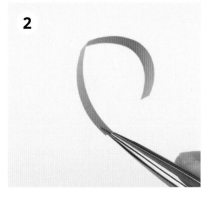

2

Make a V shape (see page 12) using pink paper. Bend one end slightly more than the other.

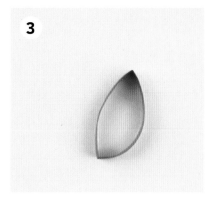

3

Apply a thin layer of glue and place it on the base.

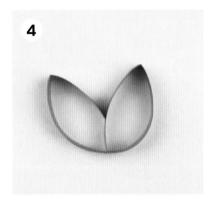

4

Make an asymmetric V shape (see page 12) using pink paper and bend both ends slightly. Apply a thin layer of glue and place it on the left side of the V shape positioned in step 2.

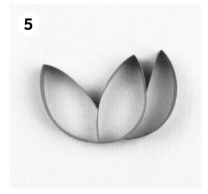

5

Make an asymmetric V shape using pink paper and bend one end slightly. Apply a thin layer of glue and place it to the right side of the V shape positioned in step 2.

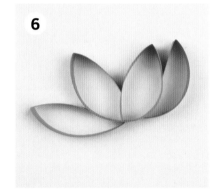

6

Make an asymmetric V shape using mint paper and bend both ends slightly. Apply a thin layer of glue and place it extending from the base of the left-hand petal.

7

Make an asymmetric V shape using mint paper and bend both ends slightly. Apply a thin layer of glue and place it extending from the base of the right-hand petals.

8

Make an asymmetric V shape using pink paper and bend one end slightly. Apply a thin layer of glue and place it on the right side of the petals.

9

Make an asymmetric V shape using pink paper and bend both ends slightly. Apply a thin layer of glue and place it on the left side of the petals.

10

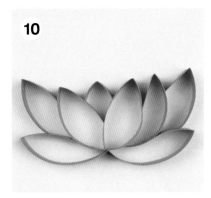

Make a V shape using pink paper and bend both ends slightly. Apply a thin layer of glue and place it between the steps 3 and 4 petals.

11

Make an asymmetric V shape using pink paper and bend both ends slightly. Apply a thin layer of glue and place it above left of the petal made in the previous step.

12

Make an asymmetric V shape using pink paper and bend both ends slightly. Apply a thin layer of glue and place it above right of the step 10 petal.

13

Make five small drop shapes (see page 14) using yellow paper. Apply a thin layer of glue and place them above the step 10 petal, towards the right side.

14

Make an asymmetric V shape using pink paper and bend both ends slightly. Apply a thin layer of glue and place it above the step 11 petal.

15

Make an asymmetric V shape using pink paper and bend both ends slightly. Apply a thin layer of glue and place it on the left side of the petal made in the previous step.

16

Make a V shape using pink paper and bend both ends slightly. Apply a thin layer of glue and place it on the right side of the step 14 petal.

17

Make an asymmetric V shape using pink paper and bend both ends slightly. Apply a thin layer of glue and place it on the right side of the petal made in the previous step.

18

Make an asymmetric V shape using pink paper and bend both ends slightly. Apply a thin layer of glue and place it above the petal made in the previous step.

19

Make an asymmetric V shape using pink paper and bend both ends slightly. Apply a thin layer of glue and place it on the right side of the petal made in the previous step.

20

Cut a piece of mint paper strip and bend it slightly. Apply a thin layer of glue and place it inside the mint coloured leaf on the left.

21

Make an asymmetric wave shape (see page 13) using white paper. Apply a thin layer of glue and place it above the shape made in the previous step.

22

Make a wave shape (see page 13) using light yellow paper. Apply a thin layer of glue and place it above the shape made in the previous step.

23

Make an asymmetric wave shape using mint paper. Apply a thin layer of glue and place it inside the mint coloured leaf on the right side.

24

Make an asymmetric wave shape using white paper. Apply a thin layer of glue and place it above the shape made in the previous step.

25

Make a wave shape using light yellow paper. Apply a thin layer of glue and place it above the shape made in the previous step.

26

Cut a piece of pink paper strip and bend it slightly. Apply a thin layer of glue and place it inside the furthest right step 8 petal.

27

Make an asymmetric wave shape using light pink paper. Apply a thin layer of glue and place it to the left side of the shape made in the previous step.

28 Cut a piece of light pink paper strip and bend it slightly. Apply a thin layer of glue and place it inside the step 5 petal (the neighbouring petal on the left).

29 Cut a piece of white paper strip, bend it slightly and cut one end so that it is rounded.

30 Apply a thin layer of glue and place it on the left side of the previously placed shape in step 28.

31 Cut a piece of pink paper strip, bend it slightly and round off one end. Apply a thin layer of glue and place it inside the neighbouring step 3 petal, on the right side.

32 Cut a piece of light pink paper strip, bend it slightly and round off one end. Apply a thin layer of glue and place it inside the same step 3 petal, on the left side.

33 Make an asymmetric wave shape using salmon pink paper. Apply a thin layer of glue and place it vertically down the centre of the same step 3 petal.

34 Cut a piece of white paper strip, bend it slightly round off one end. Apply a thin layer of glue and place it in the same petal between the steps 32 and 33 shapes.

35 Cut a piece of pink paper strip and bend it slightly. Apply a thin layer of glue and place it inside the step 4 petal on the centre left side.

36 Make a wave shape using light pink paper. Apply a thin layer of glue and place it on the right side of the shape made in the previous step.

37

Cut a piece of light pink paper strip and bend it slightly. Apply a thin layer of glue and place it on the right side of the shape made in the previous step.

38

Cut a piece of white paper strip and bend it slightly. Apply a thin layer of glue and place it on the left side of the shape made in the previous step.

39

Cut a piece of pink paper strip and bend it slightly. Apply a thin layer of glue and place it inside the far left step 9 petal.

40

Make a wave shape using light pink paper. Apply a thin layer of glue and place it on the right side of the shape made in the previous step.

41

Cut a piece of light pink paper strip and bend it slightly. Apply a thin layer of glue and place it inside the upper far left step 15 petal.

42

Make a wave shape using light pink paper. Apply a thin layer of glue and place it on the right side of the shape made in the previous step.

43

Cut a piece of light pink paper strip and bend it slightly. Apply a thin layer of glue and place it inside the neighbouring step 11 petal (towards the left side).

44

Cut a piece of light pink paper strip and bend it slightly. Apply a thin layer of glue; place it inside the step 14 petal (above the previous petal).

45

Make a wave shape using pink paper. Apply a thin layer of glue and place it inside the step 10 shape (towards the lower centre of the flower).

46

Cut a piece of light pink paper strip and bend it slightly. Apply a thin layer of glue and place it inside the step 16 petal, to the right (the petal above the yellow drop shapes).

47

Cut a piece of pink paper strip and bend it slightly. Apply a thin layer of glue and place it inside the step 12 petal, to the right (the petal to the right of the yellow drop shapes).

48

Cut a piece of light pink paper strip and bend it slightly. Apply a thin layer of glue and place it inside the step 17 petal, to the right (the petal above right of the previous step).

49

Cut a piece of light pink paper strip and bend it slightly. Apply a thin layer of glue and place it inside the step 18 petal, to the right (above the previous petal).

50

Cut a piece of light pink paper strip and bend it slightly. Apply a thin layer of glue and place it inside the step 19 petal, to the right (the top right petal).

51

Make a wave shape using light pink paper. Apply a thin layer of glue and place it to the left of the shape made in the previous step.

52

Cut a piece of salmon pink paper strip, bend it slightly and round off one end. Apply a thin layer of glue and place it inside the step 9 petal (the lower far left petal).

53

Make an asymmetric wave shape using salmon pink paper. Apply a thin layer of glue and place it inside the step 10 petal (the petal below the yellow drop shapes).

54

Make a wave shape using salmon pink paper. Apply a thin layer of glue and place it inside the step 8 petal (the lower far right petal). The flower is now complete.

Poppy

The red poppy is the birth flower for the month of August.
It symbolizes remembrance and hope for a peaceful future,
as well as imagination.

materials

- Template on page 165

- Blank sheet of 90lb (250gsm) cardstock

- 11 × ⅜in (28 × 1cm) red paper × 4

- 11 × ⅜in (28 × 1cm) black paper × 1

- 11 × ⅜in (28 × 1cm) green paper × 4

- 11 × ⅜in (28 × 1cm) emerald green paper × 1

tools

- Quilling needle or compass

- Scissors

- Tweezers

- White glue

1

To create your base, place a sheet of blank cardstock under the template, then trace the outline and lines onto it using a quilling needle or compass.

2

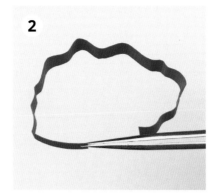

To make the first and second petals, make continuous asymmetric waves (see pages 13 and 14), similar to the shape shown, using red paper.

3

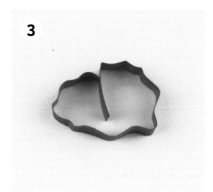

Apply a thin layer of glue and place it on the base, following the template, with the two ends in the centre, joined along part of their lengths, and leaving a gap below them.

4

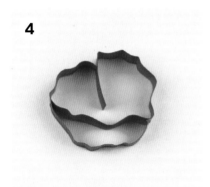

For the third petal, make a shorter continuous asymmetric wave shape using red paper and following the template. Apply a thin layer of glue; place it below the first two petals.

5

For the fourth petal, make another continuous asymmetric wave shape using red paper; follow the template. Apply a thin layer of glue and place it on the right side of the step 3 petals.

6

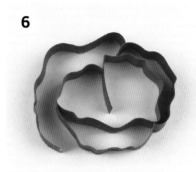

For the fifth petal, make a continuous asymmetric wave shape using red paper. Apply a thin layer of glue; place it on the left side of the petals, leaving a gap below.

7

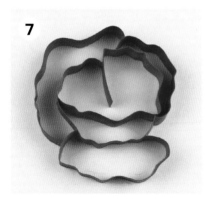

For the sixth petal, make a continuous asymmetric wave shape using red paper and the template. Apply a thin layer of glue and place it below the step 4 (third) petal.

8

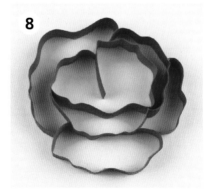

For the seventh petal, make a continuous asymmetric wave shape using red paper. Apply a thin layer of glue and place it on the right side of the step 5 (fourth) petal.

9

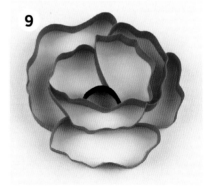

Make a C shape (see page 12) using black paper, apply a thin layer of glue and place it in the centre of the blossom, meeting the ends of the first piece.

10

Cut a 2in (5cm)-long piece of black paper and make a series of small cuts, stopping just short of the end.

11

Roll up the paper until it forms a tassel-like shape.

12

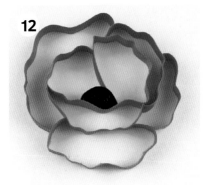

Apply a thin layer of glue along the uncut edge and place it inside the C shape made in step 9.

13

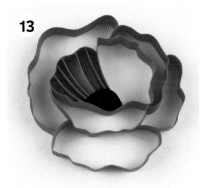

Cut five pieces of red paper and bend each one slightly. Apply a thin layer of glue and place them inside the first petal, above left of the black centre.

14

Cut six pieces of red paper and bend each one slightly. Apply a thin layer of glue and place them inside the second petal, above right of the black centre.

15

Cut eight pieces of red paper and bend each one slightly. Apply a thin layer of glue and place them inside the third petal, below the black centre.

16

Cut eight pieces of red paper and bend each one slightly. Apply a thin layer of glue and place them inside the fourth petal on the top right.

17

Cut six pieces of red paper and bend each one slightly. Apply a thin layer of glue and place them inside the seventh petal on the far right.

18

Cut 13 pieces of red paper and bend each one slightly. Apply a thin layer of glue and place them inside the fifth petal on the far left.

19

Cut ten pieces of red paper and bend each one slightly. Apply a thin layer of glue and place them inside the sixth petal at the bottom.

20

For the first stalk, slightly bend two pieces from the green paper. Apply a thin layer of glue and place them below the blossom.

21

Cut two shorter pieces of green paper and slightly bend them for a second stalk. Apply a thin layer of glue; place them just below halfway up on the right side of the stalk.

22

Using green paper, make a C-like shape on one side. Apply a thin layer of glue and place it on the left side of the stalk, continuing the top of the step 21 stalk.

23

Using green paper, repeat step 22 to make the shape. Apply a thin layer of glue and place it next to the shape made in the previous step.

24

Make an almond shape (see page 18) using green paper, apply a thin layer of glue and place it at the top end of the second stalk.

25

Make a wave shape (see page 13) using green paper. Apply a thin layer of glue; place it inside the almond shape made in the previous step.

26

Slightly bend a piece of green paper. Apply a thin layer of glue and place it next to the shape made in the previous step.

27

Make an asymmetric zigzag shape (see pages 16–17) using red paper. Apply a thin layer of glue and place it between the shapes made in steps 25 and 26.

28 Make another asymmetric zigzag shape, using green paper. Apply a thin layer of glue and place it in the bottom half of the flower bud.

29 Make another asymmetric zigzag using green paper, apply a thin layer of glue and place it in the top half of the flower bud.

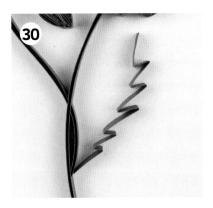

30 To form the right side of a leaf, make an asymmetric zigzag shape using green paper. Apply a thin layer of glue and place it extending from the bottom of the second stalk.

31 Using green paper, make another asymmetric zigzag shape. Apply a thin layer of glue and place it to form the left side of the leaf.

32 Slightly bend a piece of green paper, apply a thin layer of glue and place it vertically in the middle of the leaf.

33 Cut two strips of emerald green paper and slightly bend them. Apply a thin layer of glue and place them in the lower part of the left side of the leaf to form veins.

34 Cut two strips of emerald green paper and slightly bend them. Apply a thin layer of glue and place them in the upper part of the left side of the leaf, forming veins.

35 Cut two strips of emerald green paper and slightly bend them. Apply a thin layer of glue and place them in the upper part of the right side of the leaf, forming veins.

36 Finally, cut two strips of emerald green paper and slightly bend them. Apply a thin layer of glue and place them in the lower part of the right side of the leaf, forming veins.

Morning glory

September's birth flower is the morning glory. It is a symbol of love and affection. The morning glory is frequently used to express feelings of love and devotion.

materials

- Template on page 163

- Blank sheet of 90lb (250gsm) cardstock

- 1⅝ × ¼in (4 × 0.5cm) light yellow paper × 1

- 11 × ⅜in (28 × 1cm) lilac paper × 2

- 11 × ⅜in (28 × 1cm) pink paper × 1

- 11 × ⅜in (28 × 1cm) light lilac paper × 1

- 11 × ⅜in (28 × 1cm) forest green cardstock × 2

tools

- Quilling needle or compass

- Scissors

- Tweezers

- Quilling tool (optional)

- White glue

1

To create your base, place a sheet of blank cardstock under the template, then trace the outline and lines onto it using a quilling needle or compass.

2

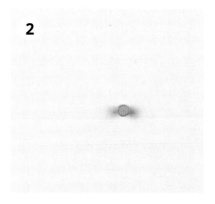

Make a tight coil (see page 11) using light yellow paper, apply a thin layer of glue and place where the centre of the lower flower should be.

3

Bend a piece of lilac paper slightly and cut one end to make it round (it will help to create a funnel shape).

4

Apply a thin layer of glue and place it on the upper left side of the yellow coil, with the rounded end next to it.

5

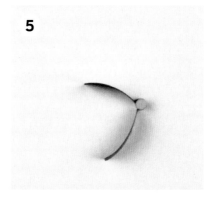

Repeat step 3. Apply a thin layer of glue and place the lilac shape on the lower left side of the yellow coil, with the rounded end next to it.

6

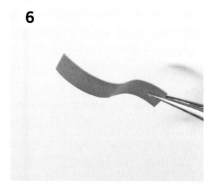

Make an asymmetric wave shape (see page 13), using lilac paper and following the template.

7

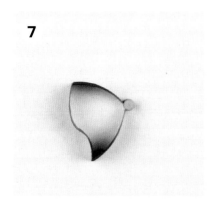

Apply a thin layer of glue and place it to connect the ends of the shapes made in steps 4 and 5.

8

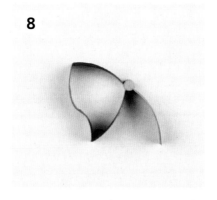

Repeat step 3. Apply a thin layer of glue to the lilac shape and place it on the lower right side of the yellow coil, with the rounded end next to it.

9

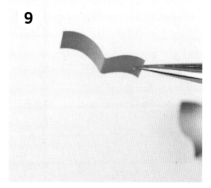

Make a V shape (see page 12) using lilac paper and curve the legs of the V, following the template.

10

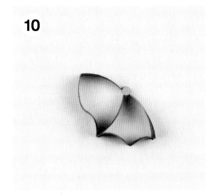

Apply a thin layer of glue and place it to connect the ends of the shapes made in steps 5 and 8.

11

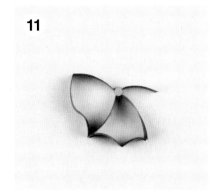

Repeat step 3. Apply a thin layer of glue and place it on the right side of the yellow coil, with the rounded end next to it.

12

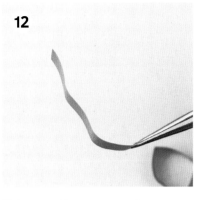

Make a continuous wave shape (see page 14) using lilac paper and following the template.

13

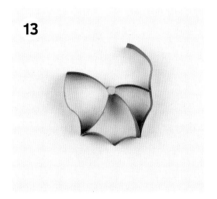

Apply a thin layer of glue and place it to connect the ends of the shapes made in steps 8 and 11, and continuing above them.

14

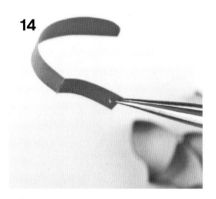

Make a V shape using lilac paper and curve the legs of the V, following the template.

15

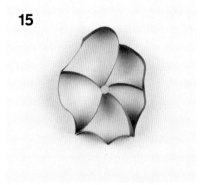

Apply a thin layer of glue and place it to form the final petal in this blossom, extending from the top of the yellow coil and meeting the step 13 and then the step 4 shapes.

16

Make a V shape using pink paper and slightly bend it. Cut both ends to round them off.

17

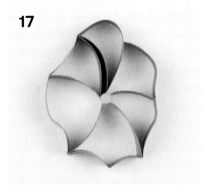

Apply a thin layer of glue and place it inside the last petal made in step 15, with the round ends next to the coil.

18

Make a V shape using pink paper and make a wave shape in the legs. Round off both ends.

19

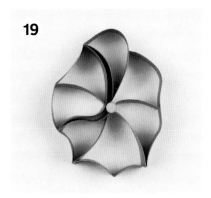

Apply a thin layer of glue and place it in the bottom left petal, with the rounded ends next to the coil.

20

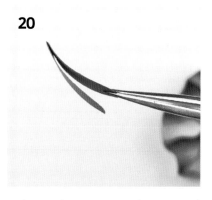

Make a V shape using pink paper and slightly bend it. Cut both ends to round them off.

21

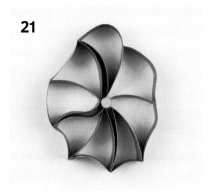

Apply a thin layer of glue and place it in the bottom petal, with the rounded ends next to the coil.

22

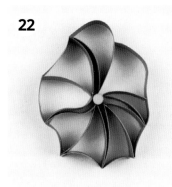

Repeat step 20, following the template for the lower right petal. Apply a thin layer of glue to the pink paper; place it in the petal with the rounded ends next to the coil.

23

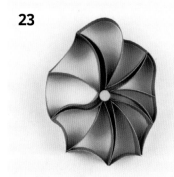

Repeat step 20, following the template for the upper right petal. Apply a thin layer of glue to the pink paper; place it in the petal with the rounded ends next to the coil.

24

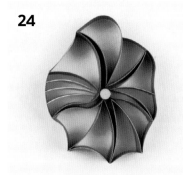

Cut three pieces of light lilac paper, slightly bend them and round off one end. Apply a layer of glue; place them in the top part of the lower left petal, with rounded ends by the coil.

25

Cut one piece of light lilac paper and cut one end to round it off; bend it to form a wave shape (see page 13).

26

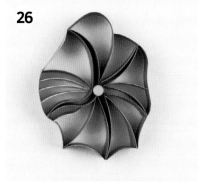

Apply a thin layer of glue and place it in the bottom part of the lower left petal, on the left-hand side, with the rounded end next to the coil.

27

Cut a piece of light lilac paper. Round off one end; slightly bend it. Apply a layer of glue; place it on the right side of the step 26 shape, with the rounded end next to the coil.

28

Cut two pieces of light lilac paper, slightly bend them and round off one end. Apply a layer of glue; place them in the left part of the bottom petal, with rounded ends by the coil.

29

Cut two pieces of light lilac paper, slightly bend them and round off one end. Apply a layer of glue; place them in the right part of the bottom petal, with rounded ends by the coil.

30

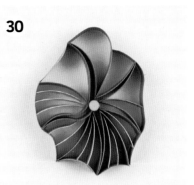

Cut a piece of light lilac paper. Round off one end; slightly bend it. Apply a layer of glue; place it in the bottom part of the lower right petal, with the rounded end next to the coil.

31

Cut a piece of light lilac paper. Round off one end; slightly bend it. Apply a layer of glue; place it in the upper part of the lower right petal, with the rounded end next to the coil.

32

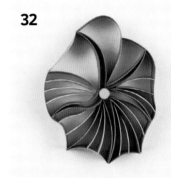

Cut a piece of light lilac paper. Round off one end; slightly bend it. Apply a layer of glue; place it in the bottom part of the upper right petal, with the rounded end next to the coil.

33

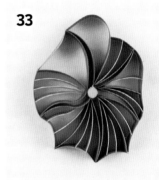

Cut a piece of light lilac paper. Round off one end; slightly bend it. Apply a layer of glue; place it in the top part of the upper right petal, with the rounded end next to the coil.

34

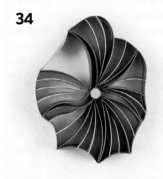

Cut two pieces of light lilac paper, slightly bend them and round off one end. Apply a layer of glue; place them in the top part of the upper left petal, with rounded ends by the coil.

35

Cut three pieces of light lilac paper, slightly bend them and round off one end. Apply a layer of glue; place them in the bottom part of the upper left petal, rounded ends by the coil.

36

Cut two strips from the forest green cardstock and bend them slightly to form a stalk. Apply a thin layer of glue and place them above the blossom, towards the left side.

37

To make the upper flower, make a continuous wave shape using lilac paper. Apply a thin layer of glue; place it to form the top of the blossom, following the template.

38

Gently bend a piece of lilac paper, apply a thin layer of glue and place it to form the right side of the flower, connect the top edge to the stalk.

39

Gently bend a piece of lilac paper, apply a thin layer of glue and place it to form the left side of the flower, connect the top edge to the stalk.

40

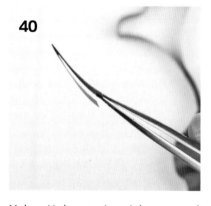

Make a V shape using pink paper and bend it slightly.

41

Apply a thin layer of glue and place it in the centre of the flower, with the open ends adjacent to the top edge.

42

Repeat step 40 to make a slightly longer pink shape. Apply a thin layer of glue and place it to the left part of the flower, with the open ends further apart next to the top edge.

43

Repeat step 42, apply the pink shape to the right side of the flower.

44

Slightly bend a piece of lilac paper, apply a thin layer of glue and place it in the far left side of the flower.

45

Slightly bend a piece of lilac paper, apply a thin layer of glue and place it to the right side of the flower, to the left of the step 43 shape.

46

Cut two strips from forest green cardstock and slightly bend for the stalk. Apply a thin layer of glue and place them below the first flower, towards the left side.

47

Make a wave shape using forest green cardstock, apply a thin layer of glue and place it to form the centre of a leaf extending from the left side of the stalk.

48

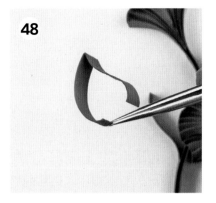

Using forest green cardstock, make a leaf by making an almond shape (see page 18) and making a wave in one side.

49

Apply a thin layer of glue and place it around the step 47 shape.

50

Using forest green cardstock, repeat first step 47, then step 48 and finally step 49 to make a second leaf shape, placing the shapes on the right side of the stalk.

51

Cut two short strips from forest green cardstock and bend them slightly. Apply a thin layer of glue; place them in the left part of the left-hand leaf to form veins.

52

Cut two short strips from forest green cardstock and bend them slightly. Apply a thin layer of glue; place them in the right part of the left-hand leaf to form veins.

53

Cut two short strips from forest green cardstock and bend them slightly. Apply a thin layer of glue; place them in the right part of the right-hand leaf to form veins.

54

Finally, cut two short strips from forest green cardstock and bend them slightly. Apply a thin layer of glue; place them in the left part of the right-hand leaf to form veins.

Cosmos

October's birth flower is the cosmos, which comes in bright colours such as pink, purple and orange. It symbolizes peace, tranquillity, order and harmony with the universe.

materials

• Template on page 162

• Blank sheet of 90lb (250gsm) cardstock

• 11 × ⅜in (28 × 1cm) 110lb (300gsm) yellow cardstock × 1

• 11 × ⅜in (28 × 1cm) 110lb (300gsm) pink cardstock × 4

tools

• Quilling needle or compass

• Scissors

• Tweezers

• Quilling crimper tool

• White glue

• Pink Copic marker pen

To create your base, place a sheet of blank cardstock under the template, then trace the outline and lines onto it using a quilling needle or compass.

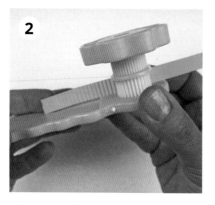

Place the yellow cardstock into the quilling crimper tool and turn it to make a crimped shape.

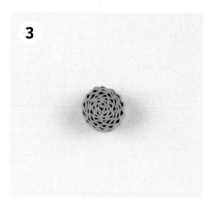

Roll up the crimped strip, apply glue to the end and place it to form the centre of the flower as indicated on the template.

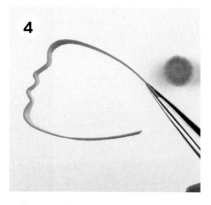

Following the template, shape a piece of pink cardstock, making asymmetric waves (see page 13) in the centre.

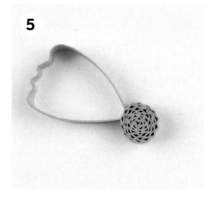

Apply a thin layer of glue and place the shape to the upper left of crimped yellow centre, with the open ends adjacent to it.

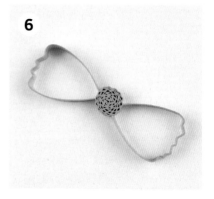

Repeat steps 4 and 5 to make a second petal, placing it opposite of the first one. You now have two whole petals – the remaining petals will overlap, so they are incomplete.

Using pink cardstock, shape a partial petal following the template. Apply a thin layer of glue; place it on the right side of the first (step 5) complete petal.

Repeat step 7 and following the template, place the new petal on the right side of the petal made in previous step.

Repeat step 7 and following the template, place the new petal on the right side of the petal made in previous step.

10

Repeat step 7 and following the template, place the new petal on the left side of the second (step 6) petal.

11

Repeat step 7 and following the template, place the new petal on the left side of the petal made in the previous step.

12

Repeat step 7 and following the template, place the final new petal on the left side of the petal made in the previous step.

13

To fill the petals, the following pink cardstock pieces vary in length. For most of them, cut one or two ends to make curves; follow the photograph for each step to place the pieces.

14

Make two pieces with a curved end and slightly bend them. Apply a layer of glue and place them inside the first (step 5) petal, near the right and left edges.

15

Make one long straight piece and two short pieces with both ends curved. Apply a thin layer of glue; place them above the previously placed left-hand piece.

16

Make two long straight pieces and one short piece with both ends curved. Apply a thin layer of glue; place them above the previously placed left-hand piece.

17

Cut one short and one longer piece, curving one end of only the short one. Apply the glue; place the short one in the left side of the adjacent petal on the right, then the long one.

18

Cut three slightly curved pieces, one of them shorter. Apply a thin layer of glue and place them on the right side of the pieces placed in the previous step – note how they are staggered.

Cut two pieces with a curved end and slightly bend them. Apply a thin layer of glue and place them to the right of the pieces placed in the previous step.

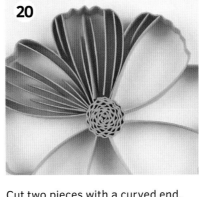

Cut two pieces with a curved end, one shorter and one longer, bending the latter one. Apply a thin layer of glue and place them in the next petal, on the left-hand side.

Cut three pieces of different lengths with a curved end. Apply a thin layer of glue and place on the right side of the pieces placed in the previous step – note how they are staggered.

Cut and bend three pink pieces of different lengths, but curve the ends of only two of them. Apply a layer of glue; place them next to the step 21 pieces, placing the straight one first.

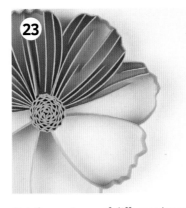

Cut three pieces of different lengths with the ends curved. Apply a thin layer of glue and place them in the next petal, in the top section.

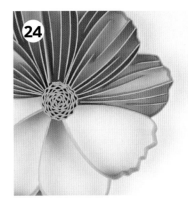

Cut three pieces in different lengths with curved ends. Apply a thin layer of glue and place them below the step 23 pieces.

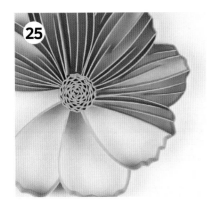

Cut three pieces of different lengths, but curve one end of only two of them. Apply a layer of glue; place them in the top of the next petal, with the straight one last.

Cut three pieces of different lengths with one end curved. Apply a thin layer of glue and place below the step 25 pieces – note how they are staggered.

Cut two pieces in different lengths, but curve an end of only one of them. Apply a thin layer of glue; place the straight one first, followed by the curved one.

Cut three pieces in different lengths with a curved end. Apply a thin layer of glue and place them in the next petal, along the right-hand side.

Cut four pieces in different lengths, but curve an end of only three of them. Apply a layer of glue; place the straight one, then the other three, staggering them, to fill the petal.

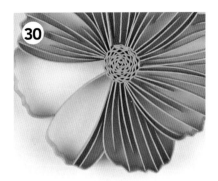

Cut two pieces in different lengths, curving an end. Apply a thin layer of glue and place them in the right side of the next petal.

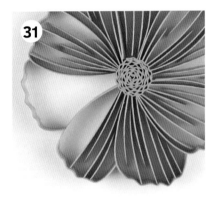

Cut two pieces in different lengths, but curve an end of only one of them. Apply a thin layer of glue; place the curved one first, followed by the straight one.

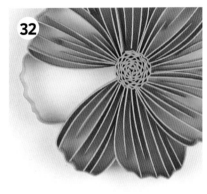

Cut two pieces in different lengths with a curved end. Apply a thin layer of glue and place them in the left-hand part of the petal.

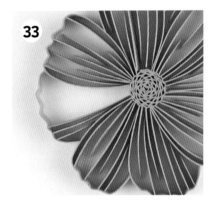

Cut three pieces in different lengths with a curved end. Apply a thin layer of glue and place them on the right-hand side of the next petal.

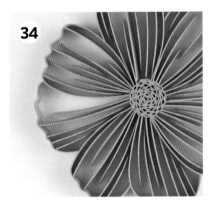

Cut two pieces in different lengths, but curve an end of only one of them. Apply a thin layer of glue; place the curved one first, followed by the straight one.

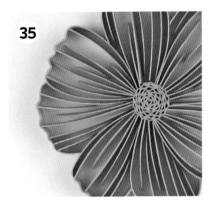

Cut two pieces in different lengths, but curve the end of only one of them. Apply a thin layer of glue; place the curved one first, followed by the straight one.

Finally, use the pink marker pen to make the petals a darker tone adjacent to the yellow centre of the flower.

Chrysanthemum

The chrysanthemum is the official flower for November birthdays. It symbolizes happiness, joy, celebration and high spirits. It is often tied to the arrival of autumn as it is one of the most popular flowers of the season.

materials

- Template on page 165

- Blank sheet of 90lb (250gsm) cardstock

- 11 × ⅜in (28 × 1cm) yellow paper × 6

- 11 × ⅜in (28 × 1cm) green paper × 2

- 11 × ⅜in (28 × 1cm) sun yellow paper × 1

tools

- Quilling needle or compass

- Scissors

- Tweezers

- White glue

1

To create your base, place a sheet of blank cardstock under the template, then trace the outline and lines onto it using a quilling needle or compass.

2

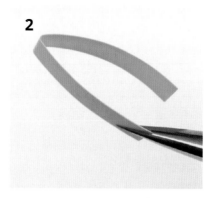

Make a V shape (see page 12) using yellow paper, then bend one end slightly inwards.

3

Apply a thin layer of glue and place it on the base paper, following the template, with the ends together to form the first petal.

4

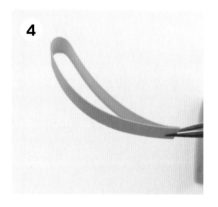

Make a bent drop shape (see page 15) using yellow paper.

5

Apply a thin layer of glue and place it on the left side of the first petal, with the ends adjacent.

6

Make another bent drop shape using yellow paper, shorter and fatter than the first. Apply a thin layer of glue and place it on the right side of the first petal.

7

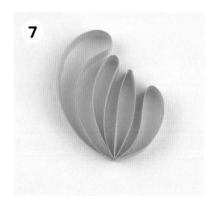

Make a larger bent drop shape using yellow paper. Apply a thin layer of glue and place it on the left side of the petals.

8

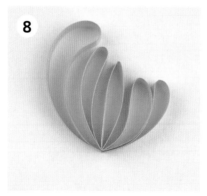

Make a shorter and thinner bent drop shape using yellow paper. Apply a thin layer of glue and place it on the right side of the petals.

9

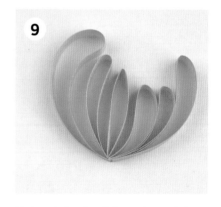

Make a taller bent drop shape using yellow paper. Apply a thin layer of glue and place it on the right side of the petals.

10

Make a similar-sized bent drop shape using yellow paper. Apply a thin layer of glue and place it on the left side of the petals.

11

Make a smaller bent drop shape using yellow paper. Apply a thin layer of glue and place it on the right side of the petals.

12

Cut two strips of green paper to form the stalk. Bend them slightly, apply a thin layer of glue and place them below the blossom.

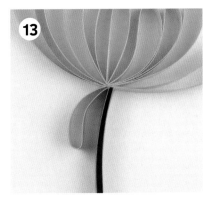

13

Make a bent drop shape using yellow paper. Apply a thin layer of glue and place it on the left side of the stalk, starting below the main flower.

14

Make a longer bent drop shape using yellow paper. Apply a thin layer of glue and place it on the left side of the petal made in the previous step.

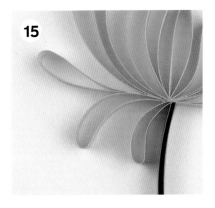

15

Make a longer bent drop shape using yellow paper. Apply a thin layer of glue; place it on the upper left side of the previously made petal step.

16

Cut a piece of yellow paper and make a wave shape (see page 13), then cut one end to round it off.

17

Apply a thin layer of glue and place it above the previously made petal.

18

Make a bent drop shape using yellow paper. Apply a thin layer of glue and place it between the petals made in steps 7 and 10.

Make a bent drop shape using yellow paper. Apply a thin layer of glue and place it between the left-hand petals made in steps 5 and 7.

Make a bent drop shape using yellow paper. Apply a thin layer of glue and place it between the left-hand petals made in steps 3 and 5.

Make a bent drop shape using yellow paper. Apply a thin layer of glue and place it on the left side of the right-hand petal made in step 9.

Make a U shape (see page 11) on one end of a piece of yellow paper.

Apply a thin layer of glue and place it on the left side of the petal made in step 21.

Cut a piece of yellow paper and bend it slightly. Apply a thin layer of glue and place it vertically below the petal made in the previous step.

Cut a piece of yellow paper and bend it slightly. Apply a thin layer of glue and place it between the first two petals made in steps 3 and 6.

Make a bent drop shape using yellow paper. Apply a thin layer of glue and place it on the left side of the shape made in the previous step.

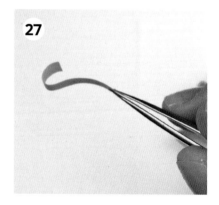

Make a U shape on the end of a piece of yellow paper and add a slight curve to the long end.

28
Apply a thin layer of glue and place it above the shape made in step 26.

29
Make a bent drop shape using yellow paper. Apply a thin layer of glue and place it between the shapes made in steps 9 and 11 (the lower two right-hand petals).

30
Make a bent drop shape using yellow paper. Apply a thin layer of glue and place it on the right side of the stalk.

31
Make a bent drop shape using yellow paper. Apply a thin layer of glue and place it on the right side of the petal made in the previous step.

32
Cut a piece of sun yellow strip and slightly bend it. Apply a thin layer of glue and place it inside the step 10 petal (on the far left).

33
Cut a piece of sun yellow strip and slightly bend it. Apply a thin layer of glue and place it inside the step 7 petal (two petals to the right of the step 32 piece).

34
Cut a piece of sun yellow strip and slightly bend it. Apply a thin layer of glue and place it inside the step 6 petal (two petals right of the centre).

35
Cut a piece of sun yellow strip and slightly bend it. Apply a thin layer of glue; place it inside the step 9 petal (two petals to the right of step 34).

36
Cut a piece of sun yellow strip and slightly bend it. Apply a thin layer of glue; place it inside the step 11 petal (two petals to the right of step 35).

37

For a leaf, make a wave shape using the green paper. Apply a thin layer of glue and place halfway up the stalk on the left-hand side.

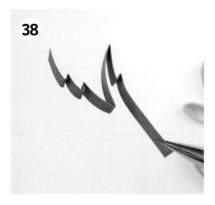

38

Make an asymmetric wave shape (see pages 16–17) using green paper, which will form the right side of the leaf.

39

Apply a thin layer of glue and place it above right of the step 37 piece.

40

Make another asymmetric wave shape using green paper, which will form the left part of the leaf.

41

Apply a thin layer of glue and place it below the step 37 piece.

42

Cut a piece of green paper strip and bend it slightly. Apply a thin layer of glue and place it in the lower left-hand part of the leaf to form a vein.

43

Cut a piece of green paper strip and bend it slightly. Apply a thin layer of glue and place it in the upper left-hand part of the leaf.

44

Cut a piece of green paper strip and bend it slightly. Apply a thin layer of glue and place it above the previously placed piece.

45

Finally, cut a piece of green paper strip and bend it slightly. Apply a thin layer of glue and place it in the right-hand part of the leaf.

Poinsettia

A winter-time favourite, poinsettia symbolizes celebration, good cheer and success. It is known as Ataturk's flower in Turkey, where it has been named after the founder of modern Turkey, who was fond of the flower.

materials

- Template on page 163
- Blank sheet of 90lb (250gsm) cardstock
- 11 × ⅜in (28 × 1cm) light yellow paper × 1
- 11 × ⅜in (28 × 1cm) yellow paper × 1
- 11 × ⅜in (28 × 1cm) red paper × 4
- 11 × ⅜in (28 × 1cm) sacramento green paper × 2

tools

- Quilling needle or compass
- Scissors
- Quilling tool (optional)
- Tweezers
- White glue

1

To create your base, place a sheet of blank cardstock under the template, then trace the outline and lines onto it using a quilling needle or compass.

2

Make seven small tight coils (see page 11) using light yellow paper and three bigger tight coils using yellow paper. Glue the coils in the centre, forming a cluster of coils.

3

Make a V shape (see page 12) using red paper; form a curve on one side and a wave (see page 13) on the other to make a bract. Apply a thin layer of glue; place it above the coils.

4

Continue to make whole bracts in a clockwise direction. Make a bigger bract using red paper; apply a thin layer of glue and place it on the upper right side of the coils.

5

Make a bigger bract using red paper, apply a thin layer of glue and place it below the coils, towards the left.

6

Make a smaller bract using red paper, apply a thin layer of glue and place it on the left side of the coils.

7

Now, following the template, make a partial bract. Apply a thin layer of glue and place it in the upper left section.

8

Following the template, make another partial bract. Apply a thin layer of glue and place it in the upper right section.

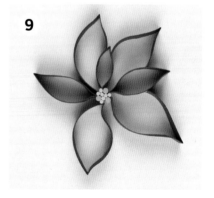

9

Following the template, make a partial bract. Apply a thin layer of glue and place it in the lower right section.

10

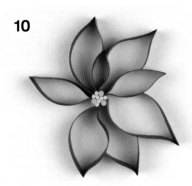

Following the template, make a partial bract. Apply a thin layer of glue and place it between the bottom and lower right bracts.

11

Following the template, make a partial bract. Apply a thin layer of glue and place it in the lower left section.

12

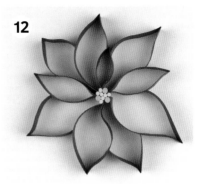

Following the template, make a partial bract. Apply a thin layer of glue and place it in the upper left section.

13

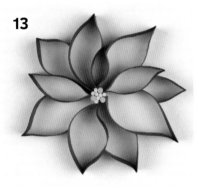

Following the template, make a partial bract. Apply a thin layer of glue and place it in between the two centre right bracts.

14

Continue in the same way to make the first partial leaf, using sacramento green paper. Apply a thin layer of glue and place it in the lower, far right section.

15

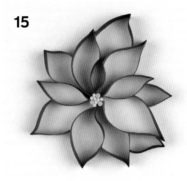

Make another partial leaf using sacramento green paper. Apply a thin layer of glue and place it in the upper right section.

16

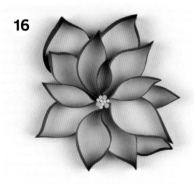

Make another partial leaf using sacramento green paper. Apply a thin layer of glue and place it in the upper left section.

17

Make another partial leaf using sacramento green paper. Apply a thin layer of glue and place it in the centre left section.

18

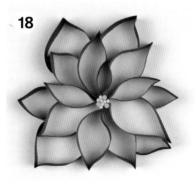

Make another partial leaf using sacramento green paper. Apply a thin layer of glue and place it in the lower left section.

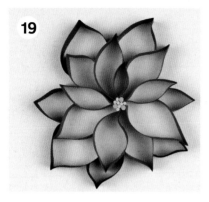

19

Make another partial leaf using sacramento green paper. Apply a thin layer of glue and place it in the bottom section.

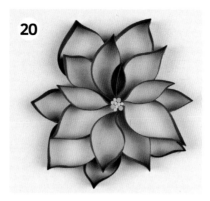

20

Next, make the details inside the bracts. Cut a short piece of red paper and slightly bend it. Apply a thin layer of glue and place it in the middle of the whole top centre bract.

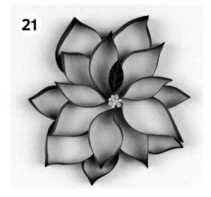

21

Cut four short pieces of red paper, apply a thin layer of glue and place them inside the step 20 bract, two on each side of the middle piece.

22

Cut a short piece of red paper and slightly bend it. Apply a thin layer of glue; place it in the middle of the adjacent partial bract on the right.

23

Cut seven short pieces of red paper, apply a thin layer of glue and place them inside the step 22 bract, two on the left of the middle piece, five on the right.

24

Cut a short piece of red paper and slightly bend it. Apply a thin layer of glue; place it in the middle of the adjacent whole bract on the right.

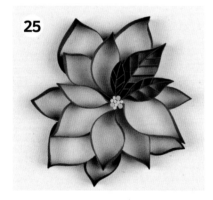

25

Cut five short pieces of red paper, apply a thin layer of glue and place them inside the step 24 bract, two above the middle piece, three below.

26

Cut a short piece of red paper and slightly bend it. Apply a thin layer of glue; place it in the middle of the larger adjacent partial bract below.

27

Cut eight short pieces of red paper, apply a thin layer of glue and place them inside the step 26 bract, three above the middle piece, five below.

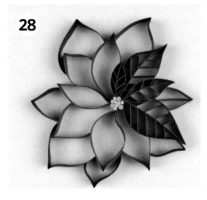

28

Cut a short piece of red paper and slightly bend it. Apply a thin layer of glue; place it in the middle of the smaller adjacent partial bract above.

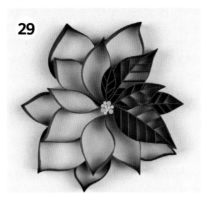

29

Cut four short pieces of red paper, apply a thin layer of glue and place them inside the step 28 bract, two on each side of the middle piece.

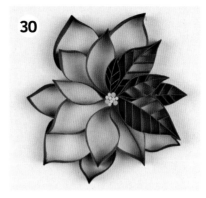

30

Cut a short piece of red paper and slightly bend it. Apply a thin layer of glue; place it in the middle of the lower right bract.

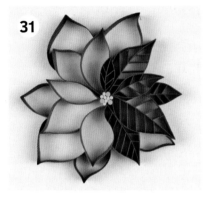

31

Cut eight short pieces of red paper, apply a thin layer of glue and place them inside the step 30 bract, two on the right of the middle piece, six on the left.

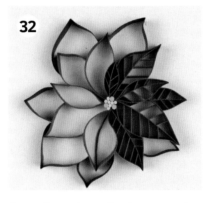

32

Cut a short piece of red paper and slightly bend it. Apply a thin layer of glue; place it in the middle of the bottom bract.

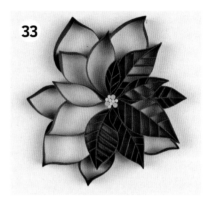

33

Cut 11 short pieces of red paper, apply a thin layer of glue and place them inside the step 32 bract, six on the right of the middle piece, five on the left.

34

Cut a short piece of red paper and slightly bend it. Apply a thin layer of glue; place it in the middle of the lower left bract.

35

Cut 11 short pieces of red paper, apply a thin layer of glue and place them inside the step 34 bract, four on the right of the middle piece, eight on the left.

36

Cut a short piece of red paper and slightly bend it. Apply a thin layer of glue; place it in the middle of the adjacent whole bract on the left.

37

Cut nine short pieces of red paper, apply a thin layer of glue and place them inside the step 36 bract, five below the middle piece, four above.

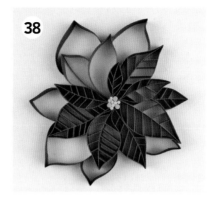

38

Cut a short piece of red paper and slightly bend it. Apply a thin layer of glue; place it in the middle of the upper left bract.

39

Cut nine short pieces of red paper, apply a thin layer of glue and place them inside the step 38 bract, five above the middle piece, four below.

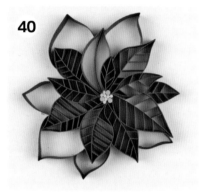

40

Cut a short piece of red paper and slightly bend it. Apply a thin layer of glue; place it in the middle of the remaining unfilled bract.

41

Cut 11 short pieces of red paper, apply a thin layer of glue and place them inside the step 40 bract, six to the left of the middle piece and five to the right.

42

Cut a short piece of sacramento green paper and slightly bend it. Apply a thin layer of glue; place it in the middle of the upper right leaf.

43

Cut four short pieces of sacramento green paper, apply a thin layer of glue and place them inside the step 42 leaf, two on each side of the middle piece.

44

Cut a short piece of sacramento green paper and slightly bend it. Apply a thin layer of glue; place it in the middle of the lower left leaf.

45

Cut four short pieces of sacramento green paper, apply a thin layer of glue and place them inside the step 44 leaf, one above the middle piece, three below.

46

Cut a short piece of sacramento green paper and slightly bend it. Apply a thin layer of glue; place it in the middle of the bottom leaf.

47

Cut seven short pieces of sacramento green paper. Apply a thin layer of glue; place them inside the step 46 leaf, two on the left of the middle piece, five on the right.

48

Cut a short piece of sacramento green paper and slightly bend it. Apply a thin layer of glue; place it in the middle of the lower left leaf.

49

Cut six short pieces of sacramento green paper. Apply a thin layer of glue; place them inside the step 48 leaf, two on the left of the middle piece, four on the right.

50

Cut a short piece of sacramento green paper and slightly bend it. Apply a thin layer of glue; place it in the middle of the leaf on the left.

51

Cut six short pieces of sacramento green paper. Apply a thin layer of glue; place them inside the step 50 leaf, three above the middle piece, three below.

52

Cut a short piece of sacramento green paper and slightly bend it. Apply a thin layer of glue; place it in the middle of the upper left leaf.

53

Cut eight short pieces of sacramento green paper. Apply a thin layer of glue; place them inside the step 52 leaf, four on the left of the middle piece, four on the right. Done!

Bird of paradise

The bird of paradise flower represents faithfulness, love, success and excellence. It is a perfect gift for someone who has just been promoted or graduated. It originates from South Africa, and it is the quintessential tropical flower.

materials

• Template on page 164

• Blank sheet of 90lb (250gsm) cardstock

• 11 × ⅜in (28 × 1cm) apple green cardstock × 1

• 11 × ⅜in (28 × 1cm) emerald green cardstock × 1

• 11 × ⅜in (28 × 1cm) red cardstock × 1

• 11 × ⅜in (28 × 1cm) dark yellow cardstock × 1

• 11 × ⅜in (28 × 1cm) indigo paper × 1

• 11 × ⅜in (28 × 1cm) crimson red paper × 1

• 11 × ⅜in (28 × 1cm) red paper × 2

• 11 × ⅜in (28 × 1cm) green cardstock × 1

tools

• Quilling needle or compass

• Scissors

• Tweezers

• Quilling tool (optional)

• White glue

1

To create your base, place a sheet of blank cardstock under the template, then trace the outline and lines onto it using a quilling needle or compass.

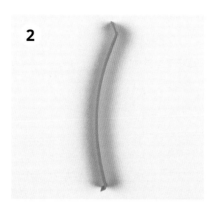

2

For the stalk, make a slightly curved shape from a piece of apple green cardstock, then bend the ends, with the bottom shorter. Apply a thin layer of glue and place on the base.

3

Make a slightly curved shape using emerald green cardstock. Apply a thin layer of glue and place it on the left side of the previous piece, between the two bent ends.

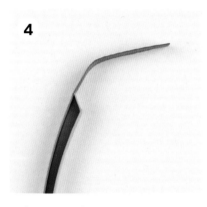

4

Make a curved shape using the red cardstock. Apply a thin layer of glue and place it as a continuation of the emerald green part below.

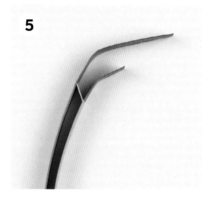

5

Make another, shorter curved shape using red cardstock. Apply a thin layer of glue and place it as a continuation of the apple green part placed in step 2.

6

Make an asymmetric V shape (see page 12) from apple green cardstock. Apply a thin layer of glue; place it with the open ends meeting the ends of the steps 4 and 5 pieces.

7

Cut a short piece from apple green cardstock, apply a thin layer of glue and place it to join the two red parts. The tip of the flower should look like a green triangle.

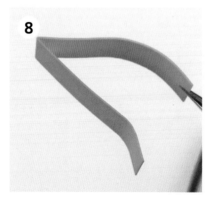

8

To make a petal-like 'tepal', create an almond shape (see page 18) using dark yellow cardstock, but curve one end outwards.

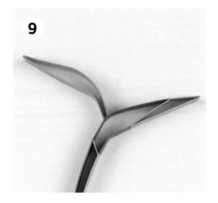

9

Apply a thin layer of glue and place the first tepal extending to the left of the step 4 red piece.

10

For the second tepal, make a wave (see page 13) in one end of an almond shape, using dark yellow cardstock. Apply a thin layer of glue; place it above the previous tepal.

11

Create a third tepal by making an almond shape using dark yellow cardstock. Apply a thin layer of glue and place on the right of the previous two tepals.

12

The fourth tepal is smaller. Using the template, create an almond-like shape using dark yellow cardstock. Apply a thin layer of glue and place to the right of the second tepal.

13

Create an almond shape using dark yellow cardstock, apply a thin layer of glue and place it to the right of the third (step 11) tepal.

14

Create a partial tepal shape from dark yellow cardstock, following the template. Apply a thin layer of glue and place it to the right of the previous tepal.

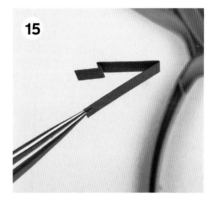

15

Make an arrow-like shape using indigo paper. First make a V shape (see page 12), then make a zigzag shape (see page 16) on one end.

16

Apply a thin layer of glue and place the indigo piece to the right of the step 14 tepal.

17

Make a similar arrow shape from another piece of indigo paper. Apply a thin layer of glue and place it between the steps 9 and 10 tepals.

18

For a leaf, make an asymmetric V shape from emerald green cardstock. Apply a thin layer of glue; place it to the left of the stalk.

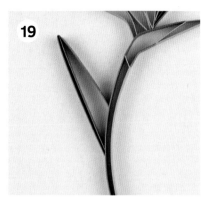

Cut a piece of emerald green cardstock, apply a thin layer of glue and place it inside the left-hand edge of the leaf.

Make a compact asymmetric zigzag shape (see pages 16–17) using the emerald green cardstock. Apply a thin layer of glue and place it inside the bottom part of the stalk.

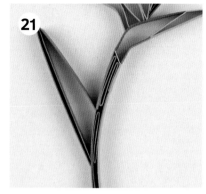

Make a compact asymmetric zigzag shape using the emerald green cardstock. Apply a thin layer of glue and place it inside the top part of the stalk.

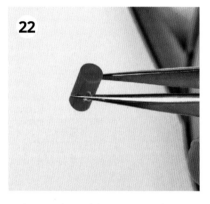

Make a tight coil (see page 11) using crimson red paper.

Make a slightly larger tight coil using red paper.

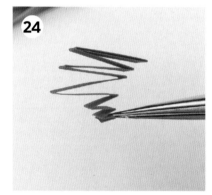

Make an asymmetric zigzag shape out of red paper, with the zigzags going from larger to smaller.

Apply a thin layer of glue; place the coils and zigzag shape in the red flower part, starting with the smaller coil and finishing with the zigzag.

Make a tight coil from red paper and a smaller tight coil from crimson red paper. Apply a thin layer of glue and place them to the right of the other coils.

Make an asymmetric zigzag shape from the apple green cardstock. Apply a thin layer of glue and place it in the triangular green section.

28

Slightly bend a piece of dark yellow cardstock, apply a thin layer of glue and place it inside the far left tepal.

29

Slightly bend the dark yellow cardstock, apply a thin layer of glue and place it inside the vertical upper left tepal.

30

Slightly bend a smaller dark yellow cardstock, apply a thin layer of glue and place it inside the tepal next to the one in the previous step.

31

Slightly bend a bigger dark yellow cardstock, apply a thin layer of glue and place it inside the tepal below the one in the previous step, along the left edge.

32

Slightly bend a smaller dark yellow cardstock, apply a thin layer of glue and place it inside the tepal on the right, along the left edge.

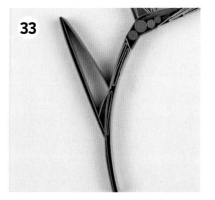

33

To finish the leaf, cut a piece of green cardstock and bend it slightly. Apply a thin layer of glue and place it in the bottom of the leaf, between the two sides.

34

Finally, following the outline of the leaf, cut and bend another 12 pieces of green cardstock, each one shorter than the previous. Apply a thin layer of glue and place them in the leaf.

Magnolia

The magnolia is considered as one of the first flowering plants to evolve on Earth. It symbolizes femininity, innocence, joy, youth and perseverance.

materials

- Template on page 164

- Blank sheet of 90lb (250gsm) cardstock

- 11 × ⅜in (28 × 1cm) orchid pink paper × 2

- 11 × ⅜in (28 × 1cm) pink paper × 2

- 11 × ⅜in (28 × 1cm) salmon pink paper × 1

- 11 × ⅜in (28 × 1cm) light pink paper × 1

- 11 × ⅜in (28 × 1cm) green paper × 1

- 11 × ⅜in (28 × 1cm) brown cardstock × 2

tools

- Quilling needle or compass

- Scissors

- Tweezers

- White glue

To create your base, place a sheet of blank cardstock under the template, then trace the outline and lines onto it using a quilling needle or compass.

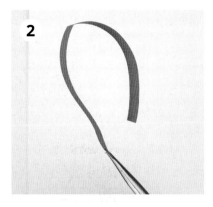

Start with the petal on the right, using orchid pink paper. Make an almond shape (see page 18), adding a wave (see page 13) on the ends.

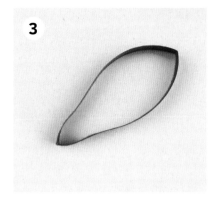

Apply a thin layer of glue and place it on the base, following the template.

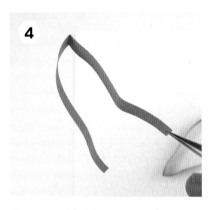

Using orchid pink paper, make another almond-like shape with waves, following the template.

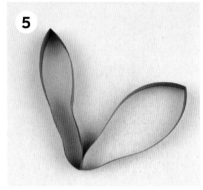

Apply a thin layer of glue and place it on the left side of the first petal.

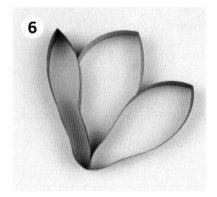

Make a V shape using pink paper, then curve the sides. Apply a thin layer of glue and place it between the first two petals.

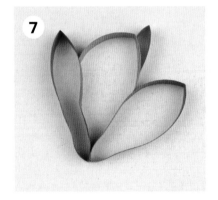

Make an asymmetric V shape (see page 12) using pink paper and curve the longer side. Apply a thin layer of glue and place it above right of the third petal in the centre.

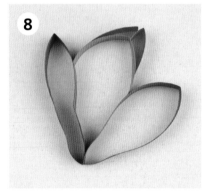

Repeat step 7 to make the shape for the opposite side of the petal, apply a thin layer of glue and place it above left of the petal in the centre.

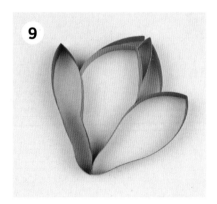

Slightly bend a piece of pink paper, apply a thin layer of glue and place it to the right of the step 7 shape.

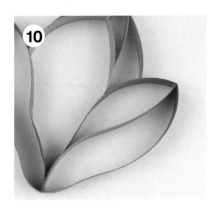

10

Make an asymmetric wave shape (see page 13) using pink paper, apply a thin layer of glue and place it inside the first right-hand petal.

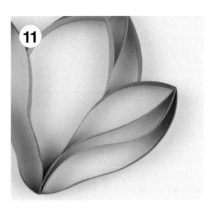

11

Make a wave shape using pink paper, apply a thin layer of glue and place it below the previously placed shape.

12

Make a wave shape using orchid pink paper, apply a thin layer of glue and place it below the previously placed shape.

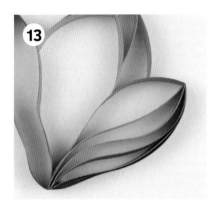

13

Slightly bend a piece of orchid pink paper strip, apply a thin layer of glue and place it below the previously placed shape.

14

Slightly bend a pink paper strip, apply a thin layer of glue and place it above the step 10 shape.

15

Slightly bend an orchid pink paper strip, apply a thin layer of glue and place it above the previously placed shape.

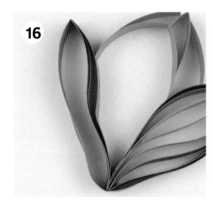

16

Make a continuous wave shape (see page 14) using orchid pink paper. Apply a thin layer of glue and place it inside the petal on the left, near the right-hand edge.

17

Make a wave shape using pink paper, apply a thin layer of glue and place it on the left side of the previously placed shape.

18

Make a continuous wave shape using pink paper, apply a thin layer of glue and place it on the left side of the previously placed shape.

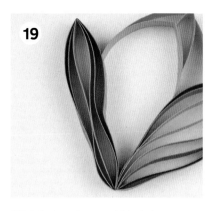

Slightly bend an orchid pink paper strip, apply a thin layer of glue and place it on the left side of the previously placed shape.

Make an asymmetric wave shape using pink paper, apply a thin layer of glue and place it inside the petal in the centre.

Make a wave shape using salmon pink paper, apply a thin layer of glue and place it on the right side of the previously placed shape.

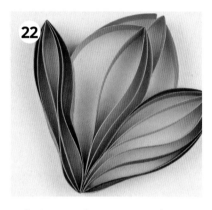

Make a wave shape using pink paper, apply a thin layer of glue and place it on the right side of the previously placed shape.

Slightly bend a pink paper strip, apply a thin layer of glue and place it on the left side of the step 20 shape.

Slightly bend a salmon pink paper strip, apply a thin layer of glue and place it on the left side of the previously placed shape.

Slightly bend a pink paper strip, apply a thin layer of glue and place it on the left side of the previously placed shape.

Slightly bend a light pink paper strip, apply a thin layer of glue and place it in the top centre right (step 7) shape.

Slightly bend a light pink paper strip, apply a thin layer of glue and place it in the adjacent shape of the right.

28

Slightly bend a light pink paper strip, apply a thin layer of glue and place it in the opposite top left shape.

29

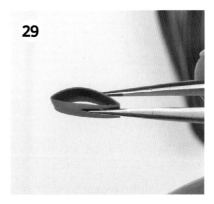

To make a leaf, form an almond shape using green paper.

30

Apply a thin layer of glue and place it below the blossom, on the left side.

31

Make another almond shape using green paper. Apply a thin layer of glue and place it below the flower, on the right side.

32

For the branch, make a continuous asymmetric wave shape (see pages 13 and 14), using brown cardstock and following the template.

33

Apply a thin layer of glue and place it extending from between the two leaves and ending towards the left, forming the left side of the branch.

34

For the upper right side, make a shorter continuous asymmetric wave shape using brown cardstock and following the template.

35

Apply a thin layer of glue and place it on the right side of the step 33 piece, starting at the pair of leaves and forming a new branch.

36

To continue the right side of the branches, make another continuous asymmetric wave shape using brown cardstock.

37

Apply a thin layer of glue and place it below the step 35 piece and to the right of the main branch (the step 33 piece).

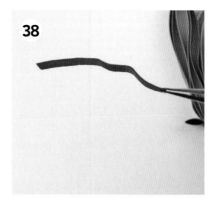

38

For the lower part of the right side of the branch, make another continuous asymmetric wave shape using brown cardstock.

39

Apply a thin layer of glue and place it below the other branch shapes, forming the bottom edge.

40

Make an almond shape, using green paper, to form a leaf.

41

Apply a thin layer of glue and place it extending from the short upper right branch.

42

Repeat step 40 to make another leaf using green paper, apply a thin layer of glue and place it extending from the short lower right branch.

43

Cut four pieces of green paper strips and bend them slightly. Apply a thin layer of glue and place one each inside the four leaf shapes.

44

Using brown cardstock, make one long continuous asymmetric wave. Apply a thin layer of glue; place it inside the main brown branch, from the leaves to the bottom left edge.

45

Finally, using the brown cardstock, make two short continuous asymmetric wave shapes. Apply a thin layer of glue and place them inside the shorter brown branches.

Lily

The white lily symbolizes a rejuvenation of the soul. It represents purity, commitment and rebirth, and is often chosen as a flower to express sympathy. It represents motherhood, a transition from one stage of life to another.

materials

- Template on page 162
- Blank sheet of 90lb (250gsm) cardstock
- 11 × ⅜in (28 × 1cm) white paper × 4
- 11 × ⅜in (28 × 1cm) lime green paper × 1
- 11 × ⅜in (28 × 1cm) yellow paper × 1

tools

- Quilling needle or compass
- Scissors
- Tweezers
- White glue
- Quilling tool (optional)

To create your base, place a sheet of blank cardstock under the template, then trace the outline and lines onto it using a quilling needle or compass.

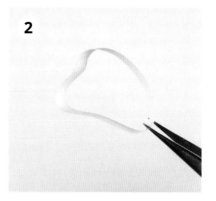

Start by making the lower right whole petal. Using white paper, make C shapes (see page 12) and waves (see page 13), following the template, with the ends curved in.

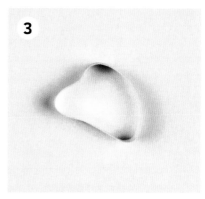

Apply a thin layer of glue and place the petal on the base, following the template.

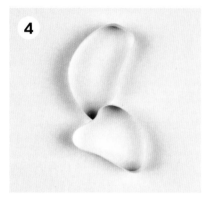

Using white paper, make a U shape (see page 11) and curves, following the template. Apply a thin layer of glue; place it above the first petal.

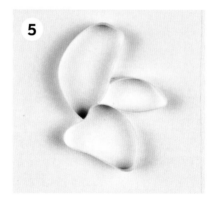

Make an almond-like shape (see page 18) using white paper. Apply a thin layer of glue and place it on the right side of the previous petal.

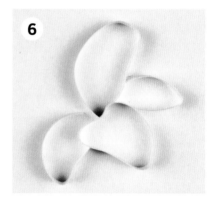

Make an almond shape, but curving only one side, using white paper. Apply a thin layer of glue and place it on the left side of the first petal, leaving a gap at the left end.

Make an almond shape using white paper. Apply a thin layer of glue and place it above the previous petal.

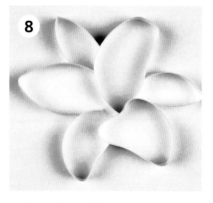

Make an almond shape using white paper. Apply a thin layer of glue and place it above the previous petal.

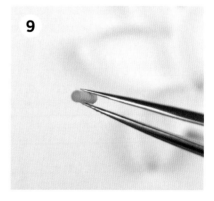

Make a tight coil (see page 11) using lime green paper.

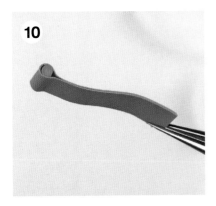

10

For the pistel, make a U shape from a lime green strip. Place the coil in the middle, apply a thin layer of glue to half the strip and press the other half over it, sealing in the coil.

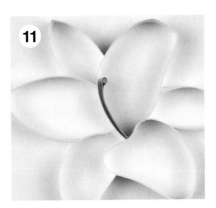

11

Apply a thin layer of glue to the edge of the piece and place it along the left-hand edge inside the second (step 4) petal.

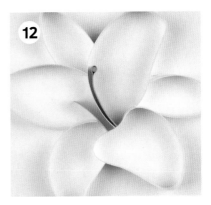

12

Bend a piece of lime green paper slightly, apply a thin layer of glue and place it by the gap left in step 6.

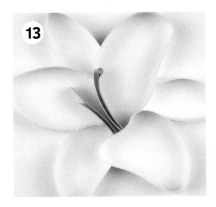

13

Bend a longer piece of lime green paper, apply a thin layer of glue and place it on the right side of the previously placed piece.

14

Make a slightly shorter wave shape from lime green paper, apply a thin layer of glue; place it on the right side of the previously placed piece.

15

Bend a slightly shorter piece of lime green paper, apply a thin layer of glue and place it on the right side of the pistel.

16

Make a slightly longer wave shape using the lime green, apply a thin layer of glue and place it on the right side of the previously placed piece.

17

Bend a slightly longer piece of lime green paper, apply a thin layer of glue and place it on the right side of the previously placed piece.

18

Make a tight coil using yellow paper, then squeeze together the opposite sides to make an oval shape. Repeat to make another five oval coils.

19

One at a time, apply a thin layer of glue to each yellow coil and place it on the end of one of the six lime green stalks.

20

Fill the petals working clockwise. Bend a piece of white paper slightly, apply a thin layer of glue and place it in the middle of the whole petal.

21

Bend a piece of white paper slightly, apply a thin layer of glue and place it on the left side of the previously placed piece.

22

Cut a piece of white paper, cutting one end into a curved shape.

23

Apply a thin layer of glue and place it on the left side of the previously placed piece.

24

Slightly bend a piece of white paper, apply a thin layer of glue and place it in the middle of the lower left petal.

25

Slightly bend another piece of white paper, apply a thin layer of glue and place it on the left side of the previously placed piece.

26

Cut a piece of white paper, curving one end. Apply a thin layer of glue and place it above the previously placed piece.

27

Slightly bend a piece of white paper, apply a thin layer of glue and place it in the centre left petal.

28

Make a second, slightly bent, but much shorter piece of white paper, apply a thin layer of glue and place it right above the previous one.

29

Cut and slightly bend a piece of white paper, apply a thin layer of glue and place in the middle of the adjacent petal.

30

Cut and slightly bend a piece of white paper, apply a thin layer of glue and place it on the right of the previously placed piece.

31

Cut and slightly bend a piece of white paper, apply a thin layer of glue and place it in the middle of the adjacent petal.

32

Cut and slightly bend a piece of white paper, apply a thin layer of glue and place it on the right of the previously placed piece.

33

Cut a piece of paper, making a curve on one end, and slightly bend it. Apply a thin layer of glue and place it on the left of the step 31 piece.

34

Cut and slightly bend a piece of white paper, apply a thin layer of glue and place it in the middle of the adjacent petal.

35

Cut and slightly bend a piece of white paper, apply a thin layer of glue and place it right below the previously placed piece.

36

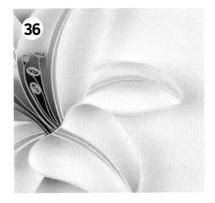

Cut a piece of paper, making a curve on one end, and slightly bend it. Apply a thin layer of glue and place it below the previously placed piece.

Tulip

One of the world's most recognizable flowers, the tulip symbolizes perfect and deep love, caring and good wishes. A tulip is the perfect gift for your partner, a friend or a member of your family.

materials

- Template on page 164
- Blank sheet of 90lb (250gsm) cardstock
- 11 × ⅜in (28 × 1cm) peach yellow paper × 1
- 11 × ⅜in (28 × 1cm) baby pink paper × 1
- 11 × ⅜in (28 × 1cm) salmon pink paper × 1
- 11 × ⅜in (28 × 1cm) pink paper × 1
- 11 × ⅜in (28 × 1cm) green paper × 1
- 11 × ⅜in (28 × 1cm) forest green paper × 1
- 11 × ⅜in (28 × 1cm) sacramento green paper × 1
- 11 × ⅜in (28 × 1cm) seafoam green paper × 1
- 11 × ⅜in (28 × 1cm) emerald green paper × 1

tools

- Quilling needle or compass
- Scissors
- Tweezers
- White glue

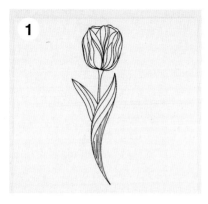

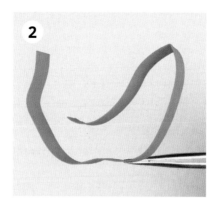

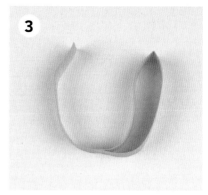

To create your base, place a sheet of blank cardstock under the template, then trace the outline and lines onto it using a quilling needle or compass.

Following the template and using peach yellow paper, first make an asymmetric V shape (see page 12), then make asymmetric waves (see page 13) and bends.

Apply a thin layer of glue and place the strip on the base following the template, with the V point at the top right and the short V side inside and adjacent to the U-like shape.

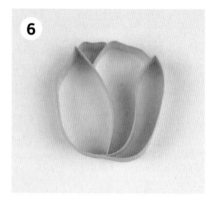

Cut and slightly bend a piece of peach yellow paper. Apply a thin layer of glue and place it to form t he left inner part of the flower.

Cut and slightly bend a piece of peach yellow paper. Apply a thin layer of glue and place it to form the upper part of the flower.

Cut and slightly bend a smaller piece of peach yellow paper. Apply a thin layer of glue and place it to form the upper left part of the flower.

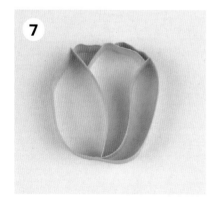

Cut and slightly bend a smaller piece of peach yellow paper. Apply a thin layer of glue and place it to form the upper right part of the flower.

Make an asymmetric wave shape using a baby pink paper strip. Apply a thin layer of glue; place it inside the left petal, near its right edge.

Make an asymmetric wave shape using a salmon pink paper strip. Apply a thin layer of glue and place it to the left side of the previously placed wave shape.

10

Make an asymmetric wave shape using baby pink paper. Apply a thin layer of glue and place it on the left side of the previously placed strip.

11

Make a wave shape using a pink paper strip, apply a thin layer of glue and place it on the left side of the previously placed strip.

12

Make a similar shape using a pink paper strip, apply a thin layer of glue and place it on the left side of the previously placed strip, but lower.

13

Cut a piece of baby pink paper and bend both ends inwards. Apply a thin layer of glue and place it on the left side of the previously placed strip.

14

Cut and slightly bend a piece of salmon pink paper. Apply a thin layer of glue and place it on the left side of the previously placed strip.

15

Make a continuous wave shape using salmon pink paper. Apply a thin layer of glue and place it on the left side of the inner right-hand edge made in step 2.

16

Make a wave shape using pink paper, apply a thin layer of glue and place it on the right side of the previously placed strip.

17

Make a continuous wave shape using baby pink paper, apply a thin layer of glue and place it on the right side of the far right edge.

18

Cut and slightly bend a strip of salmon pink paper. Apply a thin layer of glue and place it in the bottom right corner of the flower, on the right of the previously placed strip.

19

Make a continuous wave shape using baby pink paper, apply a thin layer of glue and place it between the two previously placed strips.

20

Make a wave shape using pink paper, apply a thin layer of glue and place it on the right of the previously placed strip.

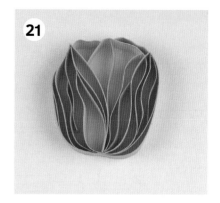

21

Make an asymmetric wave shape using salmon pink paper. Apply a thin layer of glue and place it in the middle of the flower, in the upper section.

22

Make an asymmetric wave shape from baby pink paper, apply a thin layer of glue and place it on the right side of the previously placed strip, in the upper right section of the flower.

23

Make an asymmetric wave shape from baby pink paper, apply a thin layer of glue and place it on the right side of the previously placed strip.

24

Make a slightly wavy shape using baby pink paper. Apply a thin layer of glue and place it in the centre of the upper left section of the flower.

25

Make a small wave shape using peach yellow paper. Apply a thin layer of glue and place it in the top left part of the flower.

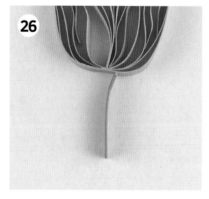

26

For the stalk, slightly bend a piece of green paper, apply a thin layer of glue and place it below the blossom.

27

Cut a slightly longer piece of green paper and slightly bend it. Apply a thin layer of glue; place it along the other green piece, on the left side.

28

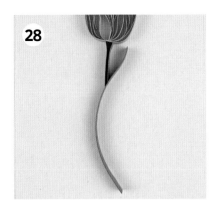

For a leaf, make an asymmetric wave shape using forest green paper. Apply a thin layer of glue and place it starting at the right of the stalk, joining both ends partway down.

29

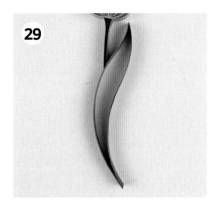

Make another asymmetric wave shape using sacramento green paper. Apply a thin layer of glue and place it on the right to form the remaining side of the leaf.

30

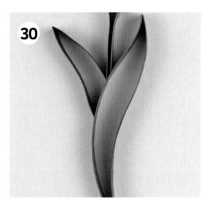

For a second leaf, make a V shape using sacramento green paper. Apply a thin layer of glue and place it to the left of the first leaf, near the bottom of the stalk.

31

Make an asymmetric wave using green paper, apply a thin layer of glue and place it inside the first leaf.

32

Make an asymmetric wave using seafoam green paper, apply a thin layer of glue and place it on the left side of the previously placed shape.

33

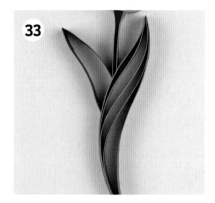

Make an asymmetric wave using green paper, apply a thin layer of glue and place it on the left side of the previously placed shape.

34

Make an asymmetric zigzag shape (see pages 16–17) using sacramento green paper. Apply a thin layer of glue; place it in the bottom right section of the first leaf.

35

Slightly bend a piece of emerald green paper, apply a thin layer of glue and place it inside the second left-hand leaf.

36

Finally, slightly bend a piece of green paper, apply a thin layer of glue and place it on the right side of the previously placed shape.

Hibiscus

The red hibiscus flower symbolizes passion, romance and love. It is the perfect flower for telling your partner how much you actually care and how passionate you are about your relationship.

materials

- Template on page 162

- 5⅛ × 5⅛ (13 × 13cm) carmine red paper for base × 1

- 11 × ⅜in (28 × 1cm) pink paper × 2

- 11 × ⅜in (28 × 1cm) carmine red paper × 3

- 11 × ⅜in (28 × 1cm) fuchsia paper × 2

- 11 × ⅜in (28 × 1cm) orange paper × 2

- 1⅛ × ⅜in (3 × 1cm) ruby red paper × 1

- 9/16 × ⅜in (1.5 × 1cm) yellow paper × 1

tools

- Quilling needle or compass

- Scissors

- Tweezers

- White glue

- Quilling tool

- Craft knife

- Cutting mat

To create your base, place a sheet of carmine red paper under the template, then trace the outline and lines onto it using a quilling needle or compass.

Start with the flower's 'style'. Make a V shape (see page 12) using pink paper and slightly curve both ends. Apply a thin layer of glue and place it on the base, following the template.

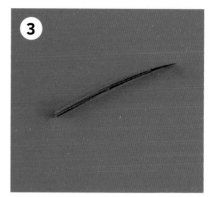

Make an asymmetric zigzag shape (see pages 16–17) using pink paper. Apply a thin layer of glue and place it to fill the style.

Start the first petal. Cut and make a continuous wave shape (see page 14) using carmine red paper. Apply a thin layer of glue; place it above the style, meeting it on the left.

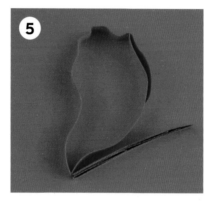

To finish this petal, make U shapes (see page 11) and wave shapes from carmine red paper. Apply a thin layer of glue; place it as shown above, with a gap between the strips on the right.

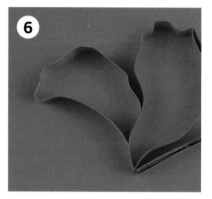

Start the second petal. Make U shapes and waves using pink paper. Apply a thin layer of glue and place it on the left side of the first petal.

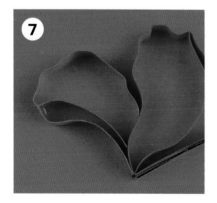

To finish the second petal, make an asymmetric wave shape (see page 13) using pink paper. Apply a thin layer of glue and place it below the previously placed piece.

Make continuous wave shapes in a piece of carmine red paper, apply a thin layer of glue and place it below the previously placed step.

Cut and slightly bend a piece of pink paper. Apply a thin layer of glue and place it below the previously placed step.

For the third petal, make continuous waves using carmine red paper. Apply a thin layer of glue and place it below the first two petals, following the template.

Make the fourth petal using carmine red paper, make first a V shape and then continuous waves. Apply a thin layer of glue and place it on the right side of the third petal.

Make an asymmetric V shape (see page 12) using carmine red paper. Apply a thin layer of glue and place it on the left side of the fourth petal.

Cut and make slight continuous waves in a piece of carmine red paper. Apply a thin layer of glue and place it on the left side of the previously placed strip.

Cut and slightly bend a piece of carmine red paper. Apply a thin layer of glue and place it on the left side of the previously placed strip.

Cut a piece of carmine red paper and make a U-like shape with waves. Apply a thin layer of glue and place it around the style made in step 2.

Cut and curve a piece of pink paper, apply a thin layer of glue and place it above the previously made shape.

Make slight wave shapes in a piece of fuchsia paper. Apply a thin layer of glue and place it inside the first petal, near the right-hand edge.

Make a slightly wavy shape using pink paper, apply a thin layer of glue and place it on the left side of the previously placed strip.

Make a wave shape using orange paper, apply a thin layer of glue and place it on the left side of the previously placed strip.

Make a wave shape using orange paper, apply a thin layer of glue and place it on the left side of the previously placed strip.

Make an asymmetric wave shape using pink paper, apply a thin layer of glue and place it on the left side of the previously placed strip.

Make an asymmetric zigzag (see pages 16–17) using orange paper. Apply a thin layer of glue and place it on the left side of the step 19 wave.

Make two shapes using pink and orange paper. Apply a thin layer of glue; place the pink shape inside the second petal, by the top, then the orange one left of the pink one.

Make an asymmetric zigzag using pink paper. Apply a thin layer of glue and place it in the upper right section of the second petal, to the right of the previously placed shape.

Make a shape following the contours of the top left edge of the third petal, using pink paper. Apply a thin layer of glue and place it inside the petal.

Make a wave shape using fuchsia paper, apply a thin layer of glue and place it in the third petal, below the previously placed shape.

Make a wave shape using carmine red paper, apply a thin layer of glue and place on the right side of the previously placed petal.

Make a wave shape using carmine red paper, apply a thin layer of glue and place it on the right side of the previously placed strip.

Cut and slightly bend a piece of orange paper. Apply a thin layer of glue and place it on the right side of the previously placed strip.

Make a slight wave-like shape using orange paper, apply a thin layer of glue and place it on the right side of the previously placed strip.

Make a wave shape using fuchsia paper. Apply a thin layer of glue and place it on the right side of the previously placed strip.

Make an asymmetric zigzag shape using fuchsia paper. Apply a thin layer of glue and fill the space created in the previous step, in the right side of the third petal.

Make an asymmetric zigzag shape using fuchsia paper. Apply a thin layer of glue and fill the space created in the previous step, in the right side of the third petal.

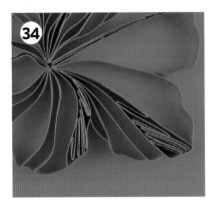

Make an asymmetric zigzag shape using pink paper. Apply a thin layer of glue and place it below the carmine red shape made in the previous step.

Make a wave shape using orange paper, apply a thin layer of glue and place it above the carmine red step 33 strip.

Make a wave shape using orange paper, apply a thin layer of glue and place it below the style, in the upper right-hand petal.

37 Make an asymmetric wave shape using carmine red paper, apply a thin layer of glue and place it below the orange shape made in the previous step.

38 Make a wave shape using fuchsia paper, apply a thin layer of glue and place it below the previous strip, above the bottom edge of the petal.

39 Make a small asymmetric V shape using ruby red paper, apply a thin layer of glue and place it at the end of the style, the ends pointing outwards, away from the style.

40 Make another small asymmetric V shape using ruby red paper, apply a thin layer of glue and place it by the previous V shape, its ends also pointing away from the style.

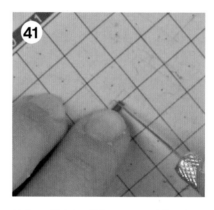

41 Make a tight coil (see page 11) using a ⅝in (1.5cm) length of ruby red paper; then cut five small pieces using a craft knife and cutting mat.

42 Apply a thin layer of glue and place the coil pieces on the tips of the small V shapes placed on the end of the style.

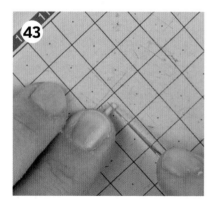

43 Make a tight coil using a ⅝in (1.5cm) length of yellow paper; then cut ten small pieces using a craft knife and cutting mat.

44 Apply a thin layer of glue and place the coil pieces on the left of the red coil pieces.

45 Finally, trim the base paper off around the flower to end up with a freestanding flower.

Lavender

The flowers of a lavender plant symbolize acceptance of all changes and challenges that come to your life. Because of its soul-soothing fragrance, people often use lavender around the home.

materials

- Template on page 163
- Blank sheet of 90lb (250gsm) cardstock
- 11 × ⅜in (28 × 1cm) royal purple paper × 5
- 11 × ⅜in (28 × 1cm) lavender paper × 4
- 11 × ⅜in (28 × 1cm) forest green cardstock × 2
- 11 × ⅜in (28 × 1cm) emerald green paper × 1

tools

- Quilling needle or compass
- Scissors
- Tweezers
- White glue
- Quilling tool (optional)

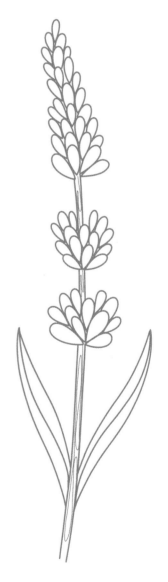

1

To create your base, place a sheet of blank cardstock under the template, then trace the outline and lines onto it using a quilling needle or compass.

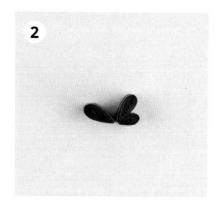

2

Make three teardrop shapes (see page 15) using royal purple paper; follow the template for the sizes. Apply a thin layer of glue; place them on the base, guided by the template.

3

Make three smaller teardrop shapes of different sizes, using lavender paper and following the template. Apply a thin layer of glue and place them around the first teardrops.

4

Make an asymmetric U shape (see page 11) using lavender paper. Apply a thin layer of glue and place it above the lavender teardrop on the left.

5

Make another asymmetric U shape using lavender paper. Apply a thin layer of glue and place it above the asymmetric U shape made in the previous step.

6

Make two teardrop shapes of different sizes using royal purple paper. Apply a thin layer of glue and place one on either side of the U shapes.

7

Using royal purple paper, make one U shape and one drop shape (see page 14). Apply a thin layer of glue; place the U shape in the upper right section, then the drop on the left.

8

Cut two pieces from forest green cardstock, one slightly longer. Apply a thin layer of glue and place them above the flower clusters, towards the centre.

9

Make four teardrop shapes: two from royal purple paper, two from lavender paper. Apply a layer of glue; place the lavender ones on the right, the royal purple ones on the left.

10

Make two asymmetric U shapes: one from lavender paper, one from royal purple. Apply a thin layer of glue; place them in the upper right area, the lavender left of the royal purple.

11

Make a teardrop shape using lavender paper. Apply a thin layer of glue and place it in the centre at the top.

12

Make two asymmetric U shapes: one from lavender paper, one from royal purple. Apply a thin layer of glue and place in the upper left section, the lavender left of the royal purple.

13

Make three teardrop shapes, one from lavender paper and two from royal purple. Apply a thin layer of glue; place the lavender on the left, the royal purple ones on the right.

14

Make two U shapes using royal purple paper. Apply a thin layer of glue; place one on the left (to the right of the last one); the other between the last two on the right.

15

Cut two pieces from forest green cardstock. Apply a thin layer of glue and place it above the flower cluster, in line with the stalk below.

16

Make one U shape using royal purple paper. Apply a thin layer of glue and place it on the left side of the green stalk made in the previous step.

17

Make three teardrops from royal purple and one teardrop from lavender paper. Apply a thin layer of glue and place them above the stalk, with the lavender third from left.

18

Make one teardrop from royal purple and one from lavender paper. Apply a thin layer of glue; place the lavender one above on the left, the royal purple one on the right.

19

Make two U shapes using royal purple paper, one smaller. Apply a thin layer of glue; place the larger one between the step 18 shapes, the other in the upper far right section.

20

Make a U shape using royal purple paper. Apply a thin layer of glue and place it above the step 19 far right shape, to the left of it.

21

Make a teardrop shape using lavender paper. Apply a thin layer of glue and place on the left side of the previously placed shape.

22

Make an asymmetric U shape using royal purple paper. Apply a thin layer of glue and place it on the left side of the previously placed shape.

23

Make two teardrops using royal purple paper. Apply a thin layer of glue and place them one on either side of the previously placed shape.

24

Make one teardrop and one U shape using lavender paper. Apply a thin layer of glue and place them above the cluster, the teardrop on the left and the U shape on the right.

25

Make two U shapes using royal purple paper, one smaller. Make one teardrop using royal purple. Apply a thin layer of glue; place them in the top layer, the teardrop in the centre.

26

Make two teardrops each from royal purple and lavender papers. Apply a thin layer of glue; from left to right, place royal purple, lavender, royal purple, lavender above the shape.

27

Make two asymmetric U shapes and one U shape using royal purple paper. Apply a thin layer of glue and place them along the top left edge, with the U shape in the middle.

28

Make one teardrop using royal purple and one teardrop using lavender paper. Apply a thin layer of glue and place them along the top left edge, with the lavender on top.

29

Make one lavender U shape, apply a thin layer of glue and place it above right of the top one placed in the previous step.

30

Make one royal purple teardrop, apply a thin layer of glue and place it above right of the one placed in the previous step.

31

To continue the stalk, cut two pieces from forest green cardstock. Apply a thin layer of glue and place them extending below the bottom cluster, in line with the stalks above.

32

Make a leaf: cut two pieces from forest green cardstock and make slight wave shapes (see page 13). Apply a thin layer of glue; place them on the left side of the stalk.

33

Repeat step 32 to make a second leaf from forest green cardstock. Apply a thin layer of glue and place the pieces on the right side of the stalk.

34

Make two wave shapes using emerald green paper. Apply a thin layer of glue and place on the inside of each leaf.

35

To fill the stalk, make asymmetric zigzag shapes (see pages 16–17), using emerald green paper, as many as you need. Apply glue to them and place them inside the stalk. Done!

Geranium

The geranium symbolizes happiness, good health, good wishes and friendship. It is associated with positive emotions, and is often given as a housewarming gift, one that brings good cheer to the home all year long.

materials

• Template on page 163

• Blank sheet of 90lb (250gsm) cardstock

• 11 × ⅜in (28 × 1cm) carmine red paper × 3

• 11 × ⅜in (28 × 1cm) orange paper × 2

• 11 × ⅜in (28 × 1cm) green paper × 2

tools

• Quilling needle or compass

• Scissors

• Tweezers

• White glue

1

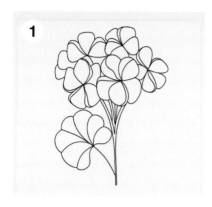

To create your base, place a sheet of blank cardstock under the template, then trace the outline and lines onto it using a quilling needle or compass.

2

Using carmine red paper, make a C shape (see page 12) continuing the curves almost to the end. Apply a thin layer of glue and place it on the base, following the template.

3

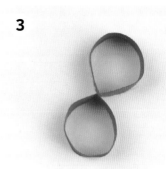

Repeat step 2 to make a similar shape from carmine red paper. Apply a thin layer of glue and place it above the first petal, with the pointed ends together.

4

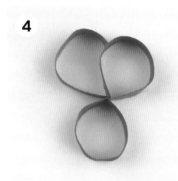

Using orange paper, make an asymmetric U shape (see page 11). Apply a thin layer of glue and place it on the left side of the step 3 shape.

5

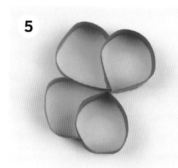

Using orange paper, make another asymmetric U shape. Apply a thin layer of glue and place below the previous shape and to the left of the step 2 shape.

6

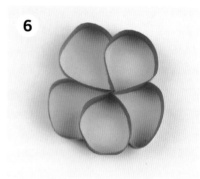

Using orange paper, make an asymmetric U shape. Apply a thin layer of glue and place it to the right side of the steps 2 and 3 shapes.

7

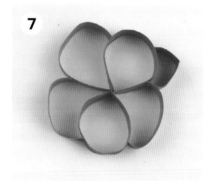

Make a V shape (see page 12) using carmine red paper and bend the ends inwards. Apply a thin layer of glue and place it to the right of the step 3 shape.

8

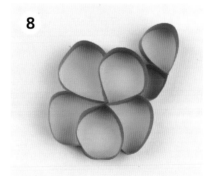

Using orange paper, make a shape similar to the step 2 shape. Apply a thin layer of glue and place it above right of the previously made step.

9

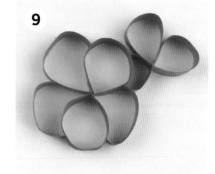

Using orange paper, repeat step 8. Apply a thin layer of glue and place it on the right side of the step 8 shape.

10

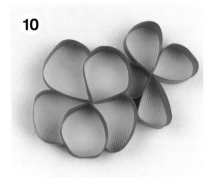

Using orange paper, repeat step 2 to make a more narrow shape. Apply a thin layer of glue and place it to the right of the step 7 shape.

11

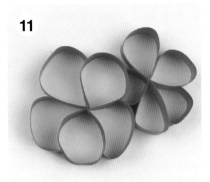

Using carmine red paper, make an asymmetric U shape. Apply a thin layer of glue and place it to the right of the previously made shape.

12

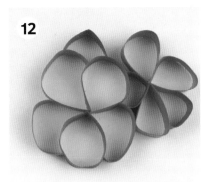

Make a V shape using carmine red paper and bend the ends inwards. Apply a thin layer of glue and place it above the steps 3 and 4 shapes on the left.

13

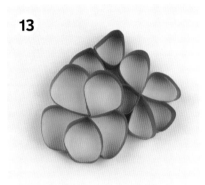

Using carmine red paper, repeat step 2 to make a similar, more squat shape. Apply a thin layer of glue and place it above right of the previously placed shape.

14

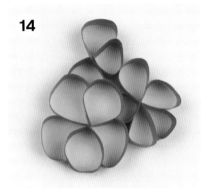

Using carmine red paper, make an asymmetric U shape. Apply a thin layer of glue and place it above left of the previously placed shape.

15

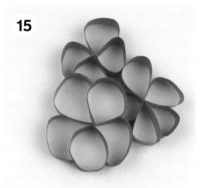

Using orange paper, make an asymmetric U shape. Apply a thin layer of glue and place it below left of the previously placed shape.

16

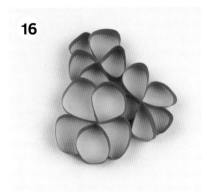

Using orange paper, make an asymmetric U shape. Apply a thin layer of glue and place it above the previously placed shape.

17

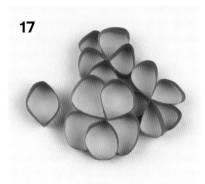

Using carmine red paper, repeat step 2 to make a similar, more almond shape. Apply a thin layer of glue and place it to the left of the cluster of petals.

18

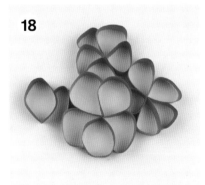

Using carmine red paper, make an asymmetric U shape. Apply a thin layer of glue and place it to the right of the previously placed shape, and bending down alongside the cluster.

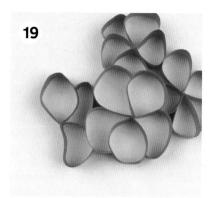

19

Using carmine red paper, make an asymmetric U shape and add a wave-like curve (see page 13). Apply a thin layer of glue; place it below the two previously placed shapes.

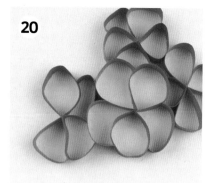

20

Using orange paper, make an asymmetric U shape. Apply a thin layer of glue and place it on the left side of the shape made in the previous step.

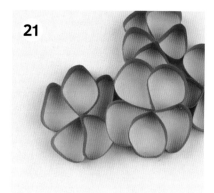

21

Using orange paper, make an asymmetric U shape. Apply a thin layer of glue; place it above left of the shape made in the previous step.

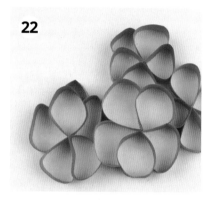

22

Using orange paper, make an asymmetric V shape. Apply a thin layer of glue and place it above the step 17 and 18 shapes.

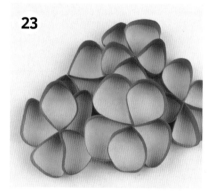

23

Using carmine red paper, make an asymmetric V shape and bend the ends inwards. Apply a thin layer of glue and place it to the left of the step 15 shape, in the upper left area.

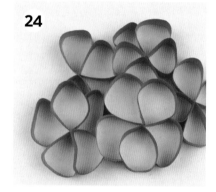

24

Using carmine red paper, make an asymmetric U shape. Apply a thin layer of glue and place it on the left side of the shape made in the previous step.

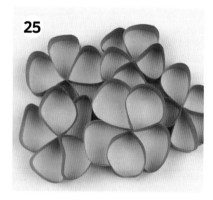

25

Using orange paper, make an asymmetric U shape. Apply a thin layer of glue and place it on the left side of the shape made in the previous step.

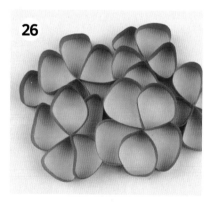

26

Using carmine red paper, make an asymmetric U shape. Apply a thin layer of glue and place it on the left side of the shape made in the previous step.

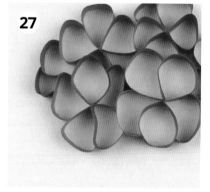

27

Using carmine red paper, make an asymmetric U shape. Apply a thin layer of glue and place it below the shape made in the previous step.

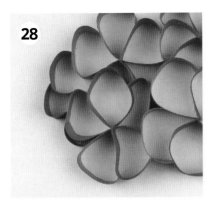

28

Cut and slightly bend a piece of orange paper strip. Apply a thin layer of glue and place it inside the step 21 petal (in the lower left area), along its bottom left edge.

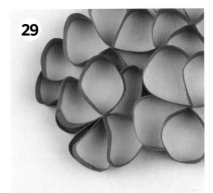

29

Cut a piece of orange paper strip and bend the end. Apply a thin layer of glue and place it inside the adjacent, below right petal, along its left edge.

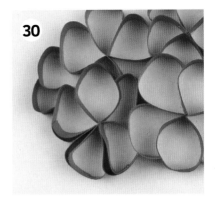

30

Cut a piece of orange paper strip and bend the end. Apply a thin layer of glue and place it inside the adjacent petal on the right, along its left edge.

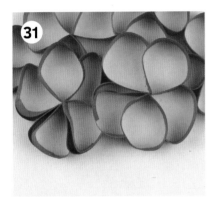

31

Cut a piece of carmine red paper strip and bend the end. Apply a thin layer of glue and place it inside the adjacent petal on the right (the step 5 petal), along its top edge.

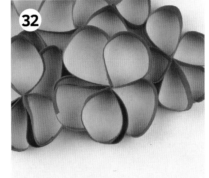

32

Cut a piece of carmine red paper strip and bend the end. Apply a thin layer of glue and place it inside the adjacent petal on the right (the step 3 petal), along its right edge.

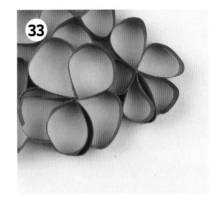

33

Cut a piece of carmine red paper strip and bend the end. Apply a thin layer of glue and place it inside the step 10 petal (in the far right section), along its right edge.

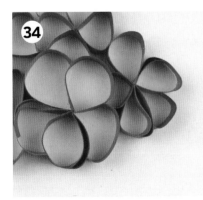

34

Cut a piece of carmine red paper strip and bend the end. Apply a thin layer of glue and place it inside the step 9 petal (in the far right section), along its right edge.

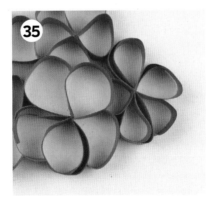

35

Cut a piece of carmine red paper strip and bend the end. Apply a thin layer of glue and place it inside the step 8 petal (in the far right section), along its left edge.

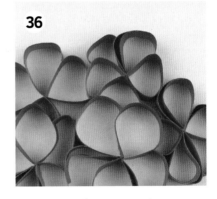

36

Cut a piece of carmine red paper strip and bend the end. Apply a thin layer of glue and place it inside the step 14 petal (in the upper right section), along its left edge.

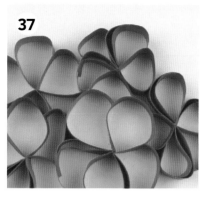

37

Cut a piece of carmine red paper strip and bend the end. Apply a thin layer of glue and place it inside the step 15 petal (in the upper right section), along its right edge.

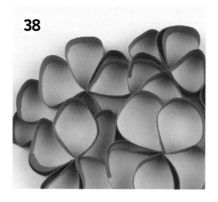

38

Cut a piece of carmine red paper strip and bend the end. Apply a thin layer of glue and place it inside the step 23 petal (in the upper left section), along its upper edge.

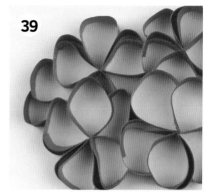

39

Make an asymmetric wave shape using carmine red paper strip. Apply a thin layer of glue and the step 25 petal (in the upper left section), along its upper edge.

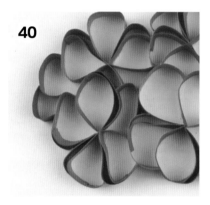

40

Cut and slightly bend a piece of carmine red paper. Apply a thin layer of glue and place it inside the step 17 petal (in the lower left section), along its right edge.

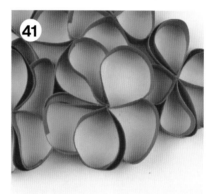

41

Make an asymmetric continuous wave shape using carmine red paper strip. Apply a thin layer of glue and place it in the middle of the step 4 petal (in the lower right section).

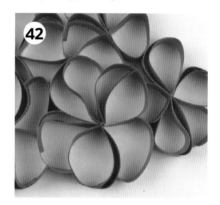

42

Cut and slightly bend a piece of carmine red paper. Apply a thin layer of glue and place it in the middle of the step 2 petal (in the lower right section).

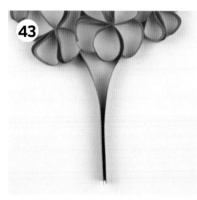

43

Start making the stalks: cut two pieces of green paper and bend them slightly. Apply a thin layer of glue; place them below the blossoms in a V shape.

44

Make an asymmetric V shape using green paper and slightly bend the ends outwards. Apply a thin layer of glue and place it between the previously placed pieces.

45

Cut a piece of green paper, following the template and slightly bending it. Apply a thin layer of glue and place it inside the right-hand stalk.

46 Cut a piece of green paper and slightly bend. Apply a thin layer of glue and place the strip in the left-hand stalk.

47 Make an asymmetric V shape using a green paper strip and slightly bend the ends outwards. Apply a thin layer of glue and place it in the centre between the two stalks.

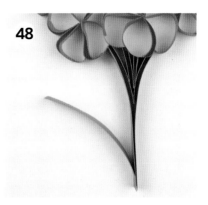

48 Cut a piece of green paper using the template and slightly bend. Apply a thin layer of glue and place it to the left side of the stem as in the photo.

49 To make the outer part of a leaf, using green paper, make a cloud-like shape following the template and using V shapes and bends. Apply a thin layer of glue.

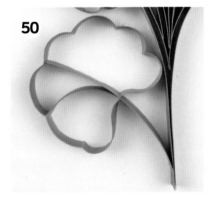

50 Place it around the free end of the step 48 shape. Cut and slightly bend a piece of green paper. Apply a layer of glue; place it in the lower part of the leaf, meeting at the point of a V.

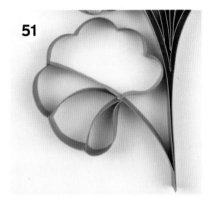

51 Cut and slightly bend another piece of green paper. Apply a thin layer of glue and place it on the right side of the previously placed piece, meeting at the point of a V shape.

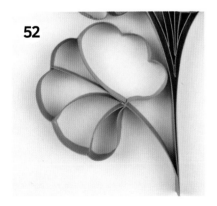

52 Cut and slightly bend a piece of green paper. Apply a thin layer of glue and place it in the upper part of the leaf, meeting at the point of a V.

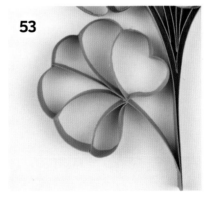

53 Cut and slightly bend a piece of green paper. Apply a thin layer of glue and place it in the upper part of the leaf, meeting at the point of a V.

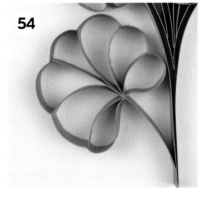

54 Finally, cut and slightly bend a piece of green paper. Apply a thin layer of glue and place it in the upper part of the leaf, meeting at the point of a V.

Sunflower

The name 'sunflower' came from its unique behaviour of facing the sun. The sunflower symbolizes loyalty, adoration and longevity. It is well-known for being a happy flower, making it the perfect gift to bring joy to someone's day.

materials

- Template on page 164
- Blank sheet of 90lb (250gsm) cardstock
- 6 × ⅜in (15 × 1cm) brown paper × 1
- 4¾ × ⅜in (12 × 1cm) chocolate brown paper × 1
- 11 × ⅜in (28 × 1cm) brown cardstock × 1
- 11 × ⅜in (28 × 1cm) light brown cardstock × 1
- 11 × ⅜in (28 × 1cm) amber paper × 1
- 11 × ⅜in (28 × 1cm) sun yellow paper × 4
- 11 × ⅜in (28 × 1cm) yellow paper × 2
- 11 × ⅜in (28 × 1cm) light yellow paper × 1
- 11 × ⅜in (28 × 1cm) forest green cardstock × 2
- 11 × ⅜in (28 × 1cm) emerald green paper × 1

tools

- Quilling needle or compass
- Scissors
- Quilling crimper tool
- Tweezers
- White glue

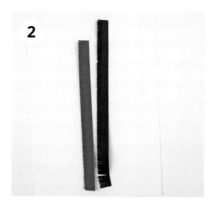

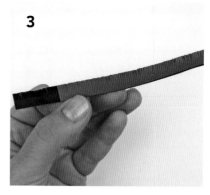

To create your base, place a sheet of blank cardstock under the template, then trace the outline and lines onto it using a quilling needle or compass.

To make tassels, make tiny cuts in a piece of 6in (15cm)-long brown paper and 4¾in (12cm)-long chocolate brown paper; take care you don't cut all the way to the end.

Glue the chocolate brown paper to the brown paper leaving a ¾in (2cm) space at one end.

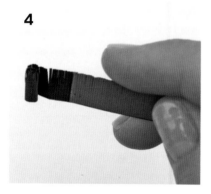

Start rolling from the brown paper.

You will have a tassel shape as shown above. Glue the end to the roll so it holds its shape.

Apply a thin layer of glue and place the tassel shape on the base, following the template.

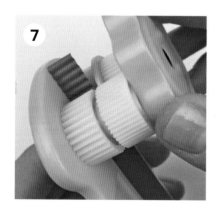

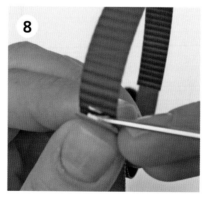

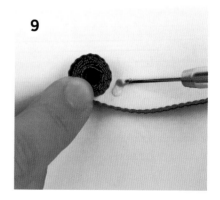

Using brown cardstock and the quilling crimper tool, make a crimped shape. Repeat with the light brown cardstock.

Glue the light brown cardstock to the end of a corresponding section of the brown cardstock, with the crimps matching, to make a longer piece of cardstock.

Wrap the crimped cardstock, starting with the brown cardstock, around the tassel shape. Apply glue to the base paper as you do, so that the cardstock stays in position.

10

The result should look like the shape above, which will be the seed section when it is complete.

11

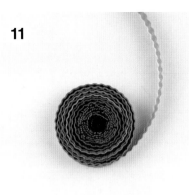

Pass the amber paper through the crimper tool. Wrap the amber paper around the tassel shape and crimped cardboard shape, applying glue as you wrap it around.

12

You will have a shape as shown above. Glue the end of the amber paper in place to finish the seed section.

13

Prepare the first petal, making an almond shape (see page 18), using the sun yellow paper.

14

Make an asymmetric V shape using sun yellow paper and curve the ends. Apply a thin layer of glue and place it to the right of the petal made in the previous step.

15

Make an asymmetric V shape using sun yellow paper and curve the ends. Apply a thin layer of glue and place it to the right of the petal made in the previous step.

16

Make an asymmetric V shape using sun yellow paper and curve the ends. Apply a thin layer of glue and place it below right of the petal made in the previous step.

17

Make an almond shape using sun yellow paper, apply a thin layer of glue and place it on the right side of the seed section.

18

Make a V shape using sun yellow paper as shown above and slightly bend it. Apply a thin layer of glue and place it between the two petals made in steps 16 and 17.

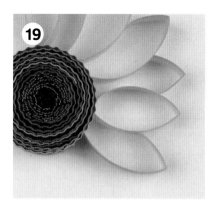

Make an asymmetric V shape using sun yellow paper and curve the ends. Apply a thin layer of glue and place it below right of the petal made in the previous step.

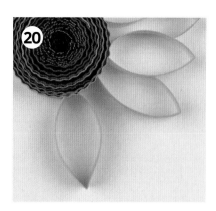

Make an almond shape using sun yellow paper, slightly bending one side of the pointed end outwards. Apply a thin layer of glue and place it below the seed section.

Make a V shape using sun yellow paper as shown above and slightly bend it. Apply a thin layer of glue and place it between the two petals made in steps 19 and 20.

Make an asymmetric V shape using sun yellow paper and curve the ends. Apply a thin layer of glue and place it to the left of the petal made in the previous step.

Make an asymmetric V shape using sun yellow paper and curve the ends. Apply a thin layer of glue and place it to the left of the petal made in the previous step.

Make an almond shape using sun yellow paper. Apply a thin layer of glue and place it to the left of the petal made in the previous step.

Make a V shape using sun yellow paper as shown above and slightly bend it. Apply a thin layer of glue and place it between the two petals made in steps 23 and 24.

Make an almond shape using sun yellow paper, slightly bending one side of the pointed end outwards. Apply a thin layer of glue and place it on the left side of the seed section.

Make an almond shape using sun yellow paper, slightly bending one side of the pointed end outwards. Apply a thin layer of glue; place it above the previously placed petal.

28

Make a V shape using sun yellow paper as shown above and slightly bend it. Apply a thin layer of glue and place it between the two petals made in steps 26 and 27.

29

Make an almond shape using sun yellow paper. Apply a thin layer of glue and place it to the right of the petal made in the previous step.

30

Make a wave shape (see page 13) using yellow paper. Apply a thin layer of glue and place it inside the first petal made (top centre), in the left-hand side.

31

Make an asymmetric wave shape (see page 13) using sun yellow paper. Apply a thin layer of glue and place it to the right of the previously made wave shape.

32

Continue to fill the petals working clockwise. Make a wave shape using yellow paper, apply a thin layer of glue and place it in the middle of the adjacent petal on the right.

33

Make a slight wave shape using yellow paper. Apply a thin layer of glue; place it in the left part of the right-hand adjacent petal.

34

Cut and slightly bend a piece of sun yellow paper. Apply a thin layer of glue and place it on the right side of the previously placed wave shape.

35

Make a wave shape using yellow paper, apply a thin layer of glue and place it in the left part of the right-hand adjacent petal.

36

Cut and slightly bend a piece of sun yellow paper. Apply a thin layer of glue and place it on the right side of the previously made wave shape.

Make a wave shape using sun yellow paper, apply a thin layer of glue and place it in the adjacent petal.

Cut and slightly bend a piece of yellow paper, apply a thin layer of glue and place it inside the adjacent petal, on the left side.

Make a wave shape using light yellow paper, apply a thin layer of glue and place it on the right of the previously placed shape.

Make a wave shape using yellow paper, apply a thin layer of glue and place it inside the adjacent petal, in the middle.

Cut and slightly bend a piece of sun yellow paper. Apply a thin layer of glue and place it on the left side of the wave shape.

Make a wave shape using yellow paper, apply a thin layer of glue and place it in the middle of the adjacent petal.

Make a wave shape using sun yellow paper, apply a thin layer of glue and place it inside the adjacent petal, near the left edge.

Cut and slightly bend a piece of sun yellow paper. Apply a thin layer of glue and place it on the left side of the wave shape.

Make a wave shape using yellow paper, apply a thin layer of glue and place it inside the adjacent petal, near the right side.

Cut and slightly bend a piece of sun yellow paper. Apply a thin layer of glue and place it on the left side of the wave shape.

Cut and slightly bend a piece of yellow paper. Apply a thin layer of glue and place it on the left side of the adjacent petal.

Make a wave shape using sun yellow paper, apply a thin layer of glue and place it on the left side of the adjacent petal.

Cut and slightly bend a piece of yellow paper. Apply a thin layer of glue and place it inside the adjacent petal, along the upper left edge.

Make a wave shape using light yellow paper, apply a thin layer of glue and place it on the right side of the previously placed shape.

Cut and slightly bend a piece of yellow paper. Apply a thin layer of glue and place it in the middle of the adjacent petal.

Make a wave shape using yellow paper, apply a thin layer of glue and place it in the middle of the adjacent petal.

Make a wave shape using yellow paper. Apply a thin layer of glue and place it inside the adjacent petal, on the right side.

Make an asymmetric wave shape using sun yellow paper. Apply a thin layer of glue and place it to the left of the wave shape.

55

Cut and slightly bend a piece of sun yellow paper, apply a thin layer of glue and place it inside the adjacent petal, on the right side.

56

Make a wave shape using light yellow paper, apply a thin layer of glue and place it to the left of the previously made shape.

57

For the stalk, cut two pieces from forest green cardstock, make one of them slightly longer. Apply a thin layer of glue and place them below the blossom.

58

For the left-hand leaf, make an asymmetric wave shape using forest green cardstock. Apply a thin layer of glue; place it extending from the stalk, to form the middle of the leaf.

59

Prepare an asymmetric wave shape using forest green cardstock, apply a thin layer of glue and place it above the previously placed shape.

60

Make a C shape (see page 12) using forest green cardstock, apply a thin layer of glue and place it to form the bottom edge of the leaf.

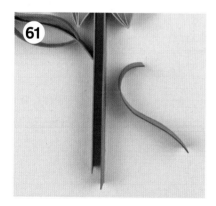

61

The next leaf has a heart shape. For the left half, using forest green cardstock, combine a C shape with a wave. Apply a thin layer of glue; place it on the right of the stalk.

62

Using forest green cardstock, repeat step 61 for the right half of the leaf. Apply a thin layer of glue and place it with the ends meeting those of the left half of the leaf.

63

Slightly bend a piece of forest green cardstock, apply a thin layer of glue and place it to the centre of the leaf.

64

Cut and slightly bend two short pieces of forest green cardstock. Apply a thin layer of glue and place them between the right-hand leaf and the stalk, joining them.

65

Cut and slightly bend two pieces of emerald green paper. Apply a thin layer of glue and place them inside the bottom area of the left-hand leaf.

66

Cut and slightly bend two pieces of emerald green paper. Apply a thin layer of glue and place them inside the upper area of the left-hand leaf.

67

Cut and slightly bend three pieces of emerald green paper, apply a thin layer of glue and place them inside the left section of the right-hand leaf.

68

Cut and slightly bend three pieces of emerald green paper. Apply a thin layer of glue and place them inside the right section of the right-hand leaf.

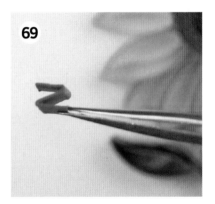

69

Make a zigzag shape (see page 16) using forest green cardstock.

70

Apply a thin layer of glue and place it in bottom of the stalk. If you also apply glue to both ends of the shape, it will stay in place better.

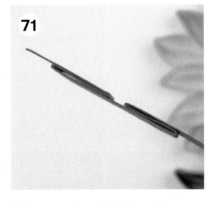

71

Make an asymmetric zigzag (see pages 16–17) using forest green cardstock. It should look like the piece shown above.

72

Finally, apply a thin layer of glue to the ends of the zigzag shape and place it inside the stalk.

Templates

All the templates are shown at actual size
and can be traced and cut out, or photocopied.

Hibiscus
page 130

Cosmos
page 82

Daffodil
page 34

Pansy
page 26

Lily
page 118

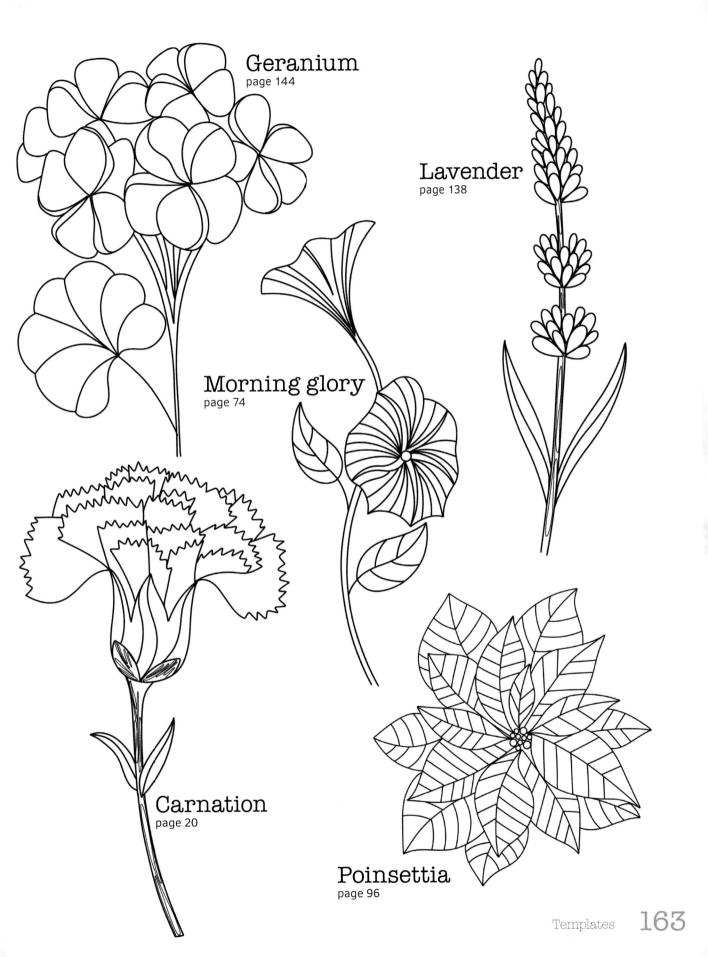

Geranium
page 144

Lavender
page 138

Morning glory
page 74

Carnation
page 20

Poinsettia
page 96

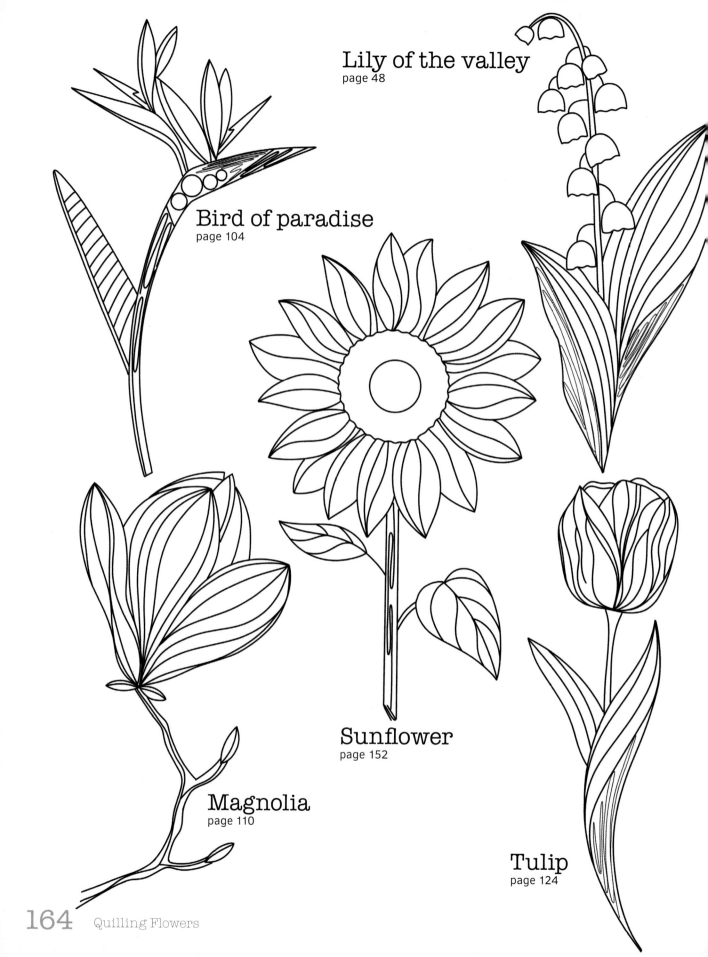

Lily of the valley
page 48

Bird of paradise
page 104

Sunflower
page 152

Magnolia
page 110

Tulip
page 124

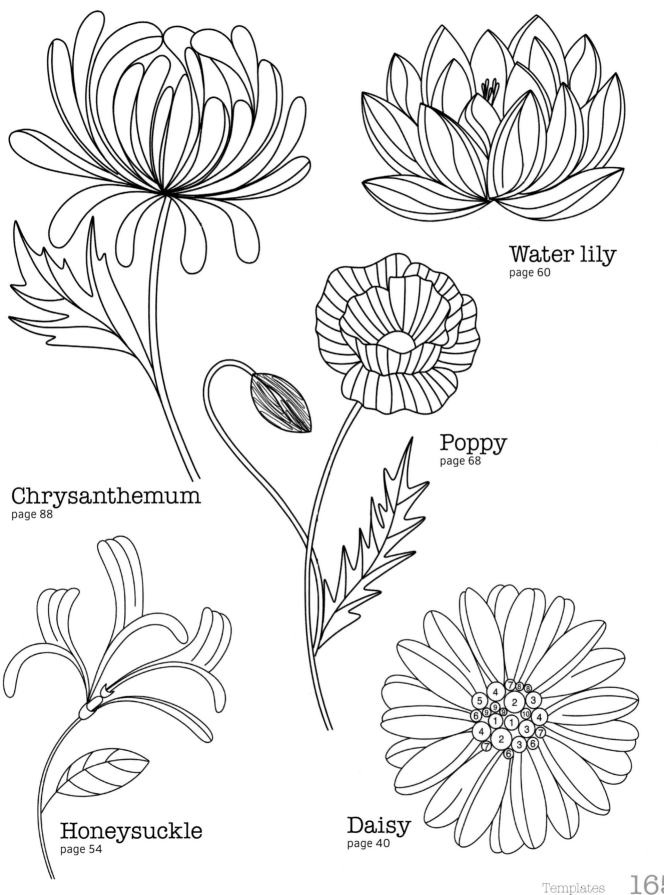

Water lily
page 60

Poppy
page 68

Chrysanthemum
page 88

Honeysuckle
page 54

Daisy
page 40

Suppliers

UK

Crafty Wizard
(Online store)
www.craftywizard.co.uk

Fred Aldous
(Online plus stores in Manchester, Leeds
and Sheffield)
www.fredaldous.co.uk

Hobbycraft
(Stores nationwide)
www.hobbycraft.co.uk

JJ Quilling Design
(Online store)
www.jjquilling.co.uk

Specialist Crafts
(Online store)
www.specialistcrafts.co.uk

The Range
(Stores nationwide)
www.therange.co.uk

USA

Jo-Ann fabric and craft
(Stores nationwide)
www.joann.com

Quilling Card
(Online store)
www.quillingcard.com

Quilled Creations
(Online store)
www.quilledcreations.com

Quilling.com
(Online store)
www.quilling.com

Walmart
(Stores nationwide)
www.walmart.com

Index

First published 2023 by
Guild of Master Craftsman Publications Ltd
Castle Place, 166 High Street, Lewes,
East Sussex, BN7 1XU, UK

ISBN 978-1-78494-656-2

The publishers and author can accept no legal
responsibility for any consequences arising from the
application of information, advice or instructions given
in this publication.

A catalogue record for this book is available from
the British Library.

Publisher: **Jonathan Bailey**
Production Manager: **Jim Bulley**
Senior Project Editors: **Tom Kitch and Sara Harper**
Editor: **Theresa Bebbington**
Design Manager: **Robin Shields**
Designer: **Rhiann Bull**
Photographer: **Andrew Perris**
Step-by-step photography: **Sena Runa**

Colour origination by GMC Reprographics
Printed and bound in China

To order a book, contact:

GMC Publications Ltd
Castle Place, 166 High Street,
Lewes, East Sussex,
BN7 1XU
United Kingdom
Tel: +44 (0)1273 488005
www.gmcbooks.com